DENISOVANS: THE GHOSTS OF THE ANCIENT WORLD

By Rayan Darcy

Origins: The Evolution of Homo Species Series

Book 4\6

Copyright © 2024 by Rayan Darcy

Table of Contents

Introduction

Welcome to "Denisovans: The Ghosts of the Ancient World," the fourth book in our series exploring the fascinating journey of human evolution. If you haven't read the first three books, "Homo habilis: The Handy Man," "Homo erectus: The First Travelers," and "Homo heidelbergensis: The Bridge to Modern Humans," we highly recommend starting there to gain a foundational understanding of the early members of the Genus Homo. Each of these books provides essential context for understanding the evolutionary advancements and adaptations that have shaped our species.

In this book, we delve into the enigmatic world of the Denisovans, a group of archaic humans whose existence was only confirmed in 2010. Through examining their technological innovations, geographic dispersal, biological changes, and social structures, we aim to shed light on their significant contributions to human evolution. The Denisovans' interactions with other hominins, their ability to adapt to diverse environments, and their enduring genetic legacy highlight their importance in our shared evolutionary history. By exploring their story, we hope to provide a comprehensive view of how these ancient humans influenced the development of our species and the intricate web of connections that bind all human beings.

Throughout this book, we will explore the various facets of Denisovan life, from their advanced tool-making skills and remarkable adaptability to their complex social behaviors and interbreeding with other hominins. By piecing together the evidence from archaeological and genetic research, we aim to reconstruct the world of the Denisovans and understand their role in the broader narrative of human evolution. This exploration will not only enhance our knowledge of these ancient humans but also provide insights into the resilience and adaptability that characterize our species.

Book Organization

Chapter 1: Denisovans Emerge

This chapter delves into the discovery and initial understanding of the Denisovans. We explore their emergence, the key fossil discoveries, and genetic analyses that have provided insight into this mysterious group of archaic humans. By examining the timeline and the significant sites where Denisovan remains have been found, we lay the groundwork for understanding their place in human evolution.

Chapter 2: Physical Characteristics

In this chapter, we examine the physical attributes of Denisovans, including their cranial capacity, facial morphology, skeletal structure, and strength. We explore their robust builds, unique dental features, and what these traits reveal about their adaptations and lifestyle.

Chapter 3: Habitat and Environment

We provide a detailed description of the climatic conditions, geography, flora, fauna, and available food resources in the habitats of Denisovans. This chapter covers the diverse environments they inhabited, from Siberia to Southeast Asia, and how they adapted to these regions.

Chapter 4: Tool Use and Technological Innovations

This chapter explores the technological advancements of Denisovans, focusing on their tool-making skills and sewing of clothes. We compare their technological innovations with those of other contemporary hominins, highlighting their contributions to early human technology.

Chapter 5: Social Structure and Behavior

An analysis of the social organization, behaviors, and cultural practices of Denisovans. We investigate evidence of social care, cooperation, and potential symbolic practices, providing a glimpse into their complex social lives.

Chapter 6: Denisovans and Us: Interbreeding

We delve into the genetic evidence of interbreeding between Denisovans and modern humans. This chapter examines the interactions between Denisovans and Homo sapiens, including friendship, competition, and interbreeding. We explore the implications of this genetic mixing, the traits inherited from Denisovans, and how these genes have persisted in modern populations.

Chapter 7: Denisovans and Neanderthals: Interbreeding

This chapter focuses on the interactions between Denisovans and Neanderthals. We explore the genetic evidence of interbreeding, the shared traits, and the evolutionary significance of their relationship.

Chapter 8: Interactions with Other Species

We explore the interactions between Denisovans and other hominin species, as well as their relationships with the animals in their environment. This chapter highlights the ecological context in which Denisovans lived and their role in their ecosystems. We also examine the animals they hunted and the predators they had to defend against, providing a comprehensive view of their survival strategies and their place in the food chain.

Chapter 9: A Story: The Mammoth Hunt

Using all that we have learned, we create a vivid narrative styled as both a novel and a documentary. We immerse you in a day in the life of a Denisovan, following a small group as they navigate the challenges of their environment. Witness their hunting expeditions, ways of caring for each other, and the thrilling pursuit of a mammoth. Grounded in scientific research, this chapter ensures that the story is both realistic and enjoyable.

Chapter 10: Role in Human Evolution

This chapter highlights the evolutionary significance of Denisovans and their contributions to later Homo species, including Homo sapiens. We discuss their role in the genetic diversity of modern humans and their place in the broader narrative of human evolution.

Chapter 11: How They Became Extinct

Finally, we discuss the various factors leading to the extinction of Denisovans, analyzing environmental changes, competition, and evolutionary pressures. We also address the ongoing research and future discoveries that may shed more light on their fate. Theories about their extinction will be explored in depth to provide a comprehensive understanding of this critical aspect of their history.

Each chapter in this book aims to provide a comprehensive understanding of Denisovans. By the end of this journey, you will have a deeper appreciation of our cousin Denisovans and their significant contributions to human evolution.

To start, we need to go back to the very beginning of the Denisovans' emergence, around 400,000 years ago.

CHAPTER I: DENISOVANS EMERGE

Discovery and Initial Insights:

The story of the Denisovans begins in the depths of the Denisova Cave, located in the rugged and remote Altai Mountains of Siberia, Russia. This cave had been a site of archaeological interest since the 1970s, but it wasn't until 2008 that a discovery would significantly alter our understanding of human evolution. Russian scientists, led by Michael Shunkov and Anatoly Derevianko from the Russian Academy of Sciences, unearthed a fragment of a finger bone from the cave. This seemingly insignificant bone fragment, belonging to a young girl, would soon reveal profound insights into the history of human species.

In 2010, geneticists led by Svante Pääbo at the Max Planck Institute for Evolutionary Anthropology in Leipzig, Germany, sequenced the mitochondrial DNA (mtDNA) from the finger bone. The results were nothing short of revolutionary. The mtDNA did not match any known human species, including Homo sapiens and Neanderthals. Instead, it indicated the existence of a previously unidentified group of archaic humans, subsequently named Denisovans after the cave where their remains were found. This discovery was monumental, suggesting a more intricate and intertwined web of human ancestry than previously understood. Genetic evidence from Denisova Cave indicated that Denisovans shared a common ancestor with Neanderthals about 400,000 to 600,000 years ago before diverging into a distinct lineage. This revelation added a new dimension to our understanding of human evolution, demonstrating that the evolutionary tree was not a simple, linear progression but a complex network of interrelated species.

Timeline and Existence:

Denisovans are believed to have existed between approximately 400,000 and 30,000 years ago, with some evidence pushing their presence as far back as 500,000 years ago. The fossils identified as Denisovan, including teeth and a jaw fragment, were discovered in various stratified layers within the Denisova Cave. These layers have been meticulously dated using advanced techniques such as optical dating, which measures the last time mineral grains were exposed to sunlight. This method has been crucial in establishing a robust timeline for Denisovan habitation, indicating that they occupied the cave for extended periods. The Denisova Cave, rich with archaeological and paleontological evidence, has provided a wealth of information about the timeline and environment of the Denisovans. The sediments within the cave contain not only Denisovan fossils but also a variety of artifacts and remains of flora and fauna. This evidence paints a comprehensive picture of the ecosystem in which Denisovans lived, suggesting that they were well-adapted to the cold, mountainous climate of the Altai region. Their ability to thrive in such challenging environments indicates a high degree of adaptability and resilience.

In addition to the Denisova Cave, Denisovan remains have been found in other locations, such as the Baishiya Karst Cave on the Tibetan Plateau. These discoveries further expand the known range of Denisovans, indicating that they were widespread across Asia. The Baishiya Karst Cave, in particular, yielded a jawbone fragment that was dated to at least 160,000 years ago, providing additional evidence of Denisovan habitation in diverse and extreme environments. The timeline established by these findings highlights the Denisovans' extensive temporal range and their ability to adapt to various climates and ecological niches. This adaptability is further underscored by genetic evidence, which shows that Denisovans interbred with both Neanderthals and modern humans, leaving a significant genetic legacy in contemporary populations, particularly in East Asia and Oceania. These interbreeding events, occurring over tens of thousands of years, underscore the Denisovans' widespread presence and their integral role in the broader story of human evolution.

Non-African Origin:

Unlike other Homo species that are prominently featured in this series, Denisovans are unique in that they are the first Homo species in this narrative that did not evolve in Africa. The Denisova Cave in Siberia and other sites in Asia are the primary locations where their remains have been found, suggesting that their evolutionary roots lie outside the African continent. This non-African origin is significant as it highlights the diversity and geographic spread of archaic human species. The evolutionary trajectory of Denisovans, separate from the African cradle of human evolution, underscores the complex nature of human ancestry and the wide-ranging migrations and adaptations of early human populations.

Why Denisovans Were Discovered So Late:

The late discovery of Denisovans in 2010 can be attributed to several factors. Firstly, the Denisova Cave and other Asian sites had not been extensively excavated or studied until relatively recently. The focus of much paleoanthropological research had traditionally been on Africa and Europe, where numerous significant finds had been made. Additionally, the preservation of fossils in these regions can be challenging due to environmental factors, leading to fewer discoveries.

Secondly, the Denisovans' identification required advanced genetic techniques that were not available until the 21st century. The sequencing of ancient DNA, particularly mitochondrial and nuclear DNA, has revolutionized the field of paleoanthropology. These genetic analyses were crucial in identifying Denisovans as a distinct group, separate from Neanderthals and modern humans. Without these techniques, the Denisovan fossils might have remained unclassified or misattributed.

Finally, the limited number of Denisovan fossils found to date has made it difficult to recognize and classify them. Unlike Neanderthals, who are represented by a wealth of skeletal remains, Denisovans are known from only a few bone fragments and teeth. This scarcity of physical evidence has posed a significant challenge to researchers, making it harder to piece together a comprehensive understanding of their physical characteristics and way of life.

Debates on Species Classification:

The classification of Denisovans has been a topic of considerable debate among scientists. Unlike Neanderthals and modern humans, Denisovans have not yet been formally assigned a distinct taxonomic name. This is primarily due to the limited number of physical remains available, which complicates the task of definitive classification. Some researchers propose that Denisovans represent a distinct species within the Homo genus, while others suggest they might be a subspecies of Homo sapiens or a regional population of Homo heidelbergensis. The debate continues as new discoveries and analyses provide more data. One of the central points of contention is the extent to which Denisovans should be considered distinct from other hominins. The genetic evidence indicates significant differences from both Neanderthals and modern humans, yet the physical evidence is sparse. This has led some scientists to advocate for caution in assigning a new species designation until more comprehensive fossil records are available. The discovery of additional Denisovan remains, particularly more complete skeletons, could provide the necessary data to resolve this debate. Until then, the Denisovans remain a fascinating yet enigmatic chapter in the story of human evolution.

Adding another layer of complexity to the Denisovan narrative is the genetic evidence suggesting the existence of multiple Denisovan lineages. Research indicates that there was significant genetic diversity among Denisovan individuals, which implies that there might have been distinct populations or lineages within this group. This genetic variation has been observed in Denisovan DNA samples from different regions, such as the Denisova Cave and the Baishiya Karst Cave on the Tibetan Plateau. The differences between these samples suggest that Denisovans were not a homogeneous group but rather a diverse and widespread population with various subgroups adapted to different environments. The idea of multiple Denisovan lineages is supported by the varied environmental contexts in which their remains have been found. The Denisova Cave, located in a cold, mountainous region, contrasts sharply with the high-altitude environment of the Tibetan Plateau. The ability of Denisovans to adapt to such diverse and extreme environments indicates a high degree of genetic and behavioral flexibility. This adaptability would have been crucial for their survival across the varied landscapes of prehistoric Asia.

Broader Impact and Ongoing Research:

 The discovery of the Denisovans has had a profound impact on our understanding of human evolution. It has revealed that the interactions between different hominin groups were far more complex than previously thought. Denisovans, along with Neanderthals and modern humans, represent a mosaic of interbreeding and genetic exchange that shaped the course of human history. This discovery has also underscored the importance of genetic research in uncovering the hidden chapters of our past, providing insights that fossils alone cannot offer. As ongoing research continues to uncover more about the Denisovans, each new finding contributes to a more detailed and nuanced picture of these ancient humans. Future discoveries, particularly those involving more complete skeletal remains and additional habitation sites, will likely provide further clarity on the Denisovan way of life, their interactions with other hominins, and their overall place in the human evolutionary tree. The work of researchers across the globe continues to piece together the story of the Denisovans, promising even more exciting revelations in the years to come.

In summary, the emergence of the Denisovans as a distinct group of archaic humans has significantly enriched our understanding of human evolution. The discovery of their remains in the Denisova Cave and other sites across Asia has revealed a complex and interconnected web of human ancestry. While debates about their classification and the possibility of multiple lineages continue, the Denisovans remain a crucial piece of the puzzle in the story of human evolution. As ongoing research and new discoveries shed more light on their existence, our understanding of these enigmatic humans will undoubtedly continue to evolve. The story of the Denisovans is far from complete, but each new discovery brings us closer to unraveling the mysteries of our ancient relatives and their impact on the world we inhabit today.

CHAPTER 2: PHYSICAL CHARACTERISTICS

Denisovans, despite the limited fossil evidence available, have provided intriguing insights into their physical characteristics through advanced genetic analysis. Unlike other archaic humans like Neanderthals and Homo sapiens, the Denisovans are primarily known through genetic data rather than an extensive fossil record. This chapter explores everything we know about the physical attributes of Denisovans, including their skin, hair, and eye color, as well as their body hair, facial and skull structure, and physiological differences across their populations. Additionally, we compare their intelligence and cognitive capabilities with those of modern humans and delve into aspects such as brain size, strength, and endurance.

Skin, Hair, and Eye Color:

Genetic evidence suggests that Denisovans, like Neanderthals, likely had a range of physical appearances. The few genes identified from Denisovan DNA indicate they may have had dark skin, hair, and eyes. This conclusion is drawn from the genetic similarities shared with populations that have these traits today. However, due to the limited number of Denisovan fossils and the fragmentary nature of their DNA samples, these inferences remain tentative and require more evidence for confirmation. The possibility exists that Denisovans, like modern humans, exhibited a range of phenotypic diversity, which would have allowed them to adapt to various environments across their wide geographic range. The diversity in skin, hair, and eye color among Denisovans would have been a significant factor in their adaptability, allowing them to thrive in different climates and conditions, from the cold, mountainous regions of Siberia to the high-altitude areas of the Tibetan Plateau.

The implications of these physical traits are profound. If Denisovans did indeed have dark skin, hair, and eyes, it suggests a level of adaptability and resilience that would have been crucial for survival in the varied and often harsh environments they inhabited. Dark skin, for instance, offers protection against ultraviolet radiation, which would have been beneficial in the high-altitude regions of the Tibetan Plateau. Similarly, dark hair and eyes could have provided additional protection against the elements and improved their ability to camouflage within their natural surroundings, aiding in both hunting and evasion of predators. The range of phenotypic traits among Denisovans indicates that, much like modern humans, they could have possessed a wide variety of appearances, helping them to adapt to different environmental pressures and climates.

Body Hair and Physiological Traits:

The Denisovan genome provides some clues about their physiological traits, including body hair. While there is no direct evidence about the extent of their body hair, it is reasonable to infer from their genetic relationship to Neanderthals and modern humans that Denisovans likely had similar body hair characteristics. Neanderthals are known to have had more body hair than modern humans, an adaptation to cold climates. Given that Denisovans lived in both cold and high-altitude environments, such as Siberia and the Tibetan Plateau, it is plausible that they also had substantial body hair to help retain warmth.

Body hair would have played a crucial role in thermoregulation, helping Denisovans to maintain their body temperature in freezing conditions. This adaptation would have been particularly important in the Altai Mountains and other cold regions where Denisovans are known to have lived. The presence of body hair also suggests that Denisovans were well-equipped to handle a range of environmental challenges, from icy winds to snowy landscapes. This trait, coupled with their robust physique, would have made Denisovans formidable survivors in their natural habitats. Their body hair would have provided insulation and protection against the elements, enhancing their ability to endure harsh climates and fluctuating temperatures. This physical trait would have been vital for their survival, ensuring that they could maintain a stable body temperature and remain active and capable in cold weather.

Physical Build and Stature:

The Denisovan fossils discovered, including teeth and a finger bone, suggest they had a robust and possibly large physical build. The size of their teeth, which are larger than those of both Neanderthals and modern humans, indicates a strong, sturdy physique adapted to their environments. This robust build would have been advantageous for survival in the harsh climates they inhabited. The jawbone found in the Baishiya Karst Cave supports the idea that Denisovans were physically robust, possibly with a muscular build similar to Neanderthals.

Denisovans' large teeth suggest a diet that included a variety of tough, fibrous foods, which would have required significant chewing power. This adaptation indicates a versatile diet and a capability to exploit a wide range of food resources, from plant materials to meat. Their robust build and muscular physique would have provided the strength necessary for hunting large game and foraging for food in challenging terrains. This physical strength, combined with their adaptability, would have made Denisovans successful predators and foragers in their ecosystems. The Denisovan build would have been well-suited to the physical demands of their environment, enabling them to carry out activities such as long-distance travel, hunting, and the construction of shelters in diverse and often difficult terrains. Their muscular build would have provided the endurance and power needed to navigate through rugged landscapes and to perform the physically demanding tasks required for their survival.

Facial and Skull Structure:

The Denisovan jawbone discovered in the Baishiya Karst Cave provides valuable insights into their facial and skull structure. This jawbone, which is robust and larger than those of Neanderthals and modern humans, suggests that Denisovans had a strong, prominent jaw. This robust jaw structure would have been well-suited to their diet, which likely included tough and fibrous foods requiring significant chewing power. The limited cranial fossils indicate that Denisovans had a large skull, which is consistent with a large brain size. The structure of their skulls, inferred from the available fossils, suggests that Denisovans had a broad face and a large cranium, similar to Neanderthals but with unique characteristics that set them apart as a distinct group.

Their broad face likely included prominent brow ridges and a wide nasal aperture, adaptations that would have been advantageous in cold climates. These features would have helped to warm the air before it reached their lungs and would have provided additional structural support for their robust jaws and teeth. The large cranium suggests that Denisovans had ample brain capacity, supporting complex cognitive functions and social behaviors. The unique combination of robust facial features and a large cranium highlights the Denisovans' distinctive place in the human evolutionary tree, blending traits of both archaic and modern humans.

Brain Size, Intelligence, and Cognitive Capabilities:

The brain size of Denisovans, inferred from their genetic relationship to Neanderthals and Homo sapiens, suggests that they had a brain capacity comparable to or even larger than that of modern humans. Neanderthals, with whom Denisovans share a common ancestor, had brain sizes that often equaled or exceeded those of Homo sapiens. This large brain size implies a significant capacity for complex thought and social behaviors. However, intelligence is not solely determined by brain size but also by the structure and organization of the brain, as well as environmental and cultural factors.

The Denisovans demonstrated advanced tool-making skills, as evidenced by artifacts found in the Denisova Cave. These tools indicate a level of technological innovation and adaptation to their environment. The genetic evidence also suggests that Denisovans, like Neanderthals, had the potential for speech and complex communication, given the similarities in genes associated with language in modern humans. This capability would have been crucial for coordinating activities such as hunting and social organization.

Comparing Denisovan intelligence to that of modern humans, it is important to consider that while Denisovans may not have developed the same level of technological and cultural complexity seen in contemporary Homo sapiens, their cognitive abilities were likely sophisticated. Denisovans' intelligence was adapted to their specific ecological and social needs, allowing them to survive and thrive in diverse environments. Their large brain size, combined with the evidence of advanced tool use and the potential for complex communication, suggests that Denisovans were highly intelligent beings capable of intricate social interactions and problem-solving.

The Denisovans' cognitive capabilities would have been influenced by their environment and lifestyle. Living in harsh climates and diverse terrains, Denisovans would have needed to develop strategies for survival that required advanced planning, coordination, and adaptation. This environment-driven intelligence underscores the idea that while Denisovans may not have reached the same level of technological sophistication as modern humans, their intelligence was well-suited to their way of life and the challenges they faced. Their ability to create tools, adapt to various environments, and potentially communicate complex ideas indicates a high level of cognitive function and social organization.

Strength and Endurance:

Denisovans likely possessed considerable physical strength and endurance, traits that would have been essential for their survival in the varied and often harsh environments they inhabited. Their robust build and muscular physique, inferred from the size of their bones and teeth, suggest that they were physically powerful. This strength would have been necessary for activities such as hunting large game, building shelters, and foraging for food over long distances.

Endurance is another critical aspect of Denisovan physiology. The ability to endure long periods of physical exertion, such as tracking prey or migrating across vast landscapes, would have been crucial. Denisovans' adaptation to high-altitude environments, like those found on the Tibetan Plateau, further indicates their remarkable endurance. Living at high altitudes requires physiological adaptations such as efficient oxygen use and enhanced cardiovascular capabilities. These adaptations would have allowed Denisovans to thrive in environments that were challenging both in terms of climate and geography.

In conclusion, the physical characteristics of Denisovans, including their skin, hair, and eye color, body hair, physical build, facial and skull structure, and physiological traits, paint a picture of a highly adaptable and resilient species. Their robust physique, coupled with significant cognitive capabilities and advanced tool-making skills, highlights their evolutionary success and their ability to navigate and survive in a wide range of environments. The unique combination of traits seen in Denisovans, from their muscular build and endurance to their large brain size and potential for complex communication, underscores their role as a crucial chapter in the human evolutionary story.

Their ability to adapt to diverse and often extreme environments, from the cold, mountainous regions of Siberia to the high-altitude plateaus of Tibet, speaks to their remarkable resilience. The genetic diversity among Denisovan populations further indicates their widespread presence and adaptability, suggesting that they were capable of thriving in various ecological niches. As we continue to uncover more about these enigmatic humans through ongoing research and new discoveries, our understanding of Denisovans and their contributions to human evolution will undoubtedly continue to deepen.

The Denisovans represent a fascinating branch of the human family tree, revealing the complexity and richness of our shared ancestry. Their interactions and interbreeding with other hominin groups, such as Neanderthals and early modern humans, have left a lasting genetic legacy in contemporary human populations, particularly in East Asia and Oceania. This legacy highlights the interconnectedness of human evolution and the profound impact that these ancient populations have had on shaping the genetic diversity of modern humans.

As scientists continue to study Denisovan remains and extract more genetic information, we can expect to gain even greater insights into their lives, behaviors, and interactions with other species. Each new discovery adds a piece to the puzzle of our ancient past, helping to create a more comprehensive picture of the Denisovans and their place in the history of human evolution. The ongoing exploration of Denisovan genetics and archaeology will undoubtedly continue to shed light on the many mysteries surrounding this intriguing and influential group of ancient humans.

CHAPTER 3:
HABITAT AND ENVIRONMENT

Denisovans inhabited a diverse range of environments across Asia, from the cold, mountainous regions of Siberia to the high-altitude plateaus of Tibet. This chapter explores the various habitats where Denisovans lived, the environmental challenges they faced, and how their adaptability and resilience enabled them to thrive in these diverse settings. Understanding the habitats and environments of Denisovans provides crucial insights into their lifestyle, survival strategies, and interactions with other species.

The Denisova Cave and Siberian Habitat:

Denisova Cave in the Altai Mountains of Siberia is the most well-known site associated with Denisovans. This cave has yielded significant archaeological and genetic evidence, providing a detailed picture of their habitat. The Altai Mountains, with their harsh, cold climate, presented numerous challenges. Winters were long and severe, with heavy snowfall and temperatures often dropping well below freezing. The landscape was characterized by rugged terrain, dense forests, and abundant wildlife, including large mammals such as woolly mammoths, bison, and reindeer. Denisovans adapted to this challenging environment by developing advanced hunting strategies and tools. They likely relied on a combination of hunting and gathering, utilizing the rich biodiversity of the region. The presence of large animal bones and stone tools in the Denisova Cave suggests that they were skilled hunters capable of taking down substantial prey. Their robust physical build would have been advantageous in these hunting activities, allowing them to exert the strength and endurance needed to track and capture large game. The Denisova Cave itself provided a sheltered habitat, protecting its inhabitants from the harshest weather conditions. The cave's interior offered a stable microclimate, with relatively constant temperatures and protection from wind and snow. The strategic location of the cave, near water sources and within a rich ecological zone, made it an ideal habitation site. The archaeological layers within the cave reveal a long history of occupation, indicating that Denisovans repeatedly used this site over thousands of years.

The Tibetan Plateau and High-Altitude Adaptations:

Another significant Denisovan habitat was the Tibetan Plateau, a region known for its extreme altitude and challenging living conditions. The discovery of a Denisovan jawbone in the Baishiya Karst Cave at an elevation of over 3,200 meters (10,500 feet) above sea level suggests that Denisovans were remarkably adaptable to high-altitude environments. The Tibetan Plateau is one of the most inhospitable places on Earth, with low oxygen levels, intense ultraviolet radiation, and significant temperature fluctuations between day and night. Denisovans' ability to thrive at such high altitudes points to several physiological adaptations. Genetic studies have identified specific alleles in modern Tibetan populations, inherited from Denisovans, that contribute to high-altitude adaptation. These genetic traits include enhanced oxygen transport and utilization, which would have been crucial for survival in an environment with thin air. The Denisovans' robust physical build and possible physiological traits such as increased lung capacity and efficient blood circulation would have further supported their high-altitude lifestyle. The Tibetan Plateau's environment also influenced Denisovan subsistence strategies. The region's flora and fauna were unique, with high-altitude plants and animals forming the basis of their diet. The presence of yak bones and other high-altitude fauna in the Baishiya Karst Cave suggests that Denisovans adapted their hunting and gathering practices to exploit the available resources. Their ability to process and utilize these resources indicates a high level of ecological knowledge and skill.

Food Sources and Diet:

Denisovans had a varied diet that reflected the diversity of their habitats. In the cold, mountainous regions of Siberia, their diet likely included large mammals such as woolly mammoths, bison, and reindeer. These animals provided a rich source of protein and fat, which would have been essential for survival in the harsh climate. The presence of large animal bones in the Denisova Cave suggests that Denisovans were skilled hunters capable of taking down substantial prey. These large mammals would have been hunted using advanced tools and cooperative hunting strategies, allowing Denisovans to secure large quantities of meat that could be shared among group members and preserved for future use. In addition to large mammals, Denisovans would have consumed smaller animals, fish, and a variety of plant materials. Smaller game such as hares, birds, and fish would have supplemented their diet, providing additional sources of protein and nutrients. The variety of bones and artifacts found in Denisovan sites indicates that they were adept at exploiting a wide range of animal resources. The inclusion of fish in their diet suggests that Denisovans had developed fishing techniques, likely using tools made from bone or wood to catch fish from rivers and streams. Plant materials would have been another important component of the Denisovan diet. Berries, nuts, tubers, and other plant foods would have been gathered seasonally, providing essential vitamins and minerals that complemented their meat-based diet. The gathering of plant materials would have required a detailed knowledge of the local flora, including which plants were edible and how to prepare them for consumption. This knowledge would have been passed down through generations, ensuring that Denisovans could make the most of the available plant resources. In the high-altitude regions of the Tibetan Plateau, Denisovans would have hunted high-altitude fauna such as yaks and other local animals. The ability to hunt and process these animals indicates that Denisovans were well-adapted to their environment and possessed advanced hunting skills. The dietary flexibility of Denisovans underscores their evolutionary success and resilience in diverse habitats. Their ability to adapt their diet to the available resources would have been crucial for their survival, allowing them to thrive in a variety of ecological niches across Asia.

Water Sources and Settlement Patterns:

Access to reliable water sources was crucial for Denisovan survival. In the Altai Mountains, rivers and streams provided essential water for drinking, cooking, and processing food. The strategic location of the Denisova Cave near water sources made it an ideal habitation site. The availability of water also influenced settlement patterns, with Denisovans likely establishing camps and habitation sites near reliable water sources. These water sources would have been vital for daily life, providing not only drinking water but also resources for cooking and cleaning. On the Tibetan Plateau, the high-altitude environment would have posed additional challenges in accessing water. Glacial meltwater and high-altitude lakes would have been primary sources of water. The presence of the Baishiya Karst Cave near water sources indicates that Denisovans strategically chose their habitation sites to ensure access to water. The ability to locate and utilize water sources would have been a critical survival skill, enabling Denisovans to establish stable and sustainable settlements in challenging environments. Settlement patterns would have been influenced by the availability of food and water, as well as the need for shelter from harsh weather conditions. Denisovans likely moved seasonally, following the migration patterns of animals and the seasonal availability of plant resources. This seasonal movement would have required detailed knowledge of the landscape and its resources, allowing Denisovans to plan their movements and establish temporary or semi-permanent camps in areas that provided the best opportunities for survival.

Geographical Range and Migration Patterns:

The Denisovan geographical range was extensive, covering a wide area across Asia. Genetic evidence from modern human populations suggests that Denisovans interbred with early Homo sapiens in Southeast Asia and Oceania, indicating a broader geographic range than initially understood. This wide distribution points to the Denisovans' remarkable adaptability and ability to thrive in diverse habitats, from tropical forests to coastal regions. Denisovans likely migrated across vast distances, following the movement of animals and changes in climate. These migrations would have taken them through a variety of environments, from the cold, mountainous regions of Siberia to the warm, tropical forests of Southeast Asia. The ability to migrate and adapt to different environments highlights the Denisovans' resilience and versatility as a species. Their interactions with other hominin groups, including Neanderthals and early modern humans, would have facilitated genetic exchange and the spread of Denisovan traits across a broad geographic area. The coastal regions of Southeast Asia and Oceania would have offered abundant marine resources, including fish, shellfish, and other seafood. The exploitation of these resources would have required specialized tools and techniques, further highlighting the Denisovans' ingenuity and adaptability. The genetic legacy of Denisovans in these regions, particularly among indigenous populations, provides a testament to their extensive range and successful integration into diverse ecosystems.

Environmental Challenges and Survival Strategies:

Denisovans faced immense environmental challenges across their habitats, which ranged from the freezing terrains of Siberia to the high-altitude extremes of the Tibetan Plateau, and even to the tropical conditions of Southeast Asia. Each of these environments posed unique survival difficulties, requiring Denisovans to develop specialized adaptations and strategies to thrive.

Living in Siberia meant enduring long, brutal winters with temperatures that could plummet well below freezing. The landscape was a mix of dense forests and rugged terrain, making travel and hunting physically demanding. The Denisova Cave, where many Denisovan artifacts have been found, provided some shelter from the elements. However, surviving in this environment required more than just shelter. Denisovans needed to maintain their body heat, which they likely did through the use of animal skins for clothing and constructing well-insulated shelters. The cold also made finding food challenging, as many plants were not available during the winter months, and animals were harder to track and hunt.

The Tibetan Plateau presented another set of challenges with its extreme altitudes, often exceeding 3,000 meters above sea level. The air is thin at these altitudes, making it difficult to breathe and increasing the risk of altitude sickness. Denisovans had to adapt physiologically to survive in such conditions. Genetic evidence suggests that Denisovans possessed specific adaptations that allowed them to use oxygen more efficiently, a trait that modern populations in the region have inherited. The high UV radiation levels also posed a threat, requiring Denisovans to develop protective measures, possibly through clothing or behavioral adaptations like limiting exposure during peak sunlight hours.

In contrast to the cold and high-altitude regions, the tropical forests of Southeast Asia posed different challenges, such as high humidity, heat, and the presence of various diseases. Denisovans had to contend with dense vegetation, which made hunting and gathering more complex and energy-intensive. The constant threat of tropical diseases would have required a robust immune system and knowledge of medicinal plants to treat illnesses. The availability of diverse food sources in tropical regions meant that Denisovans needed extensive knowledge of edible plants and animals, but the competition with other species for these resources would have been fierce.

Across all these environments, Denisovans had to navigate and adapt to the diverse landscapes and climates. This required a high degree of mobility and flexibility in their survival strategies. Seasonal migrations were likely a part of their lifestyle, moving to different areas to exploit seasonal food sources and avoid the harshest conditions. This nomadic lifestyle required a deep understanding of the geography and ecology of their territories, as well as the ability to transport resources and maintain social cohesion within their groups.

The ability to survive in such challenging environments also depended on social and technological adaptations. Denisovans likely relied heavily on social structures for cooperative hunting, shared knowledge, and mutual support during times of scarcity. Technological innovations, such as advanced tool-making, would have been critical in improving their efficiency in hunting, processing food, and constructing shelters. The development and use of tools from available materials like bone, wood, and stone reflect their ingenuity and adaptability.

In conclusion, the Denisovans' environments were fraught with challenges that required a combination of physical, social, and technological adaptations to overcome. Their ability to endure and thrive in such harsh and varied climates speaks to their remarkable resilience and ingenuity. The study of Denisovan habitats and survival strategies provides a window into the incredible adaptability of ancient human populations and their capacity to innovate and cooperate in the face of extreme environmental pressures.

CHAPTER 4:
TOOL USE AND INNOVATION

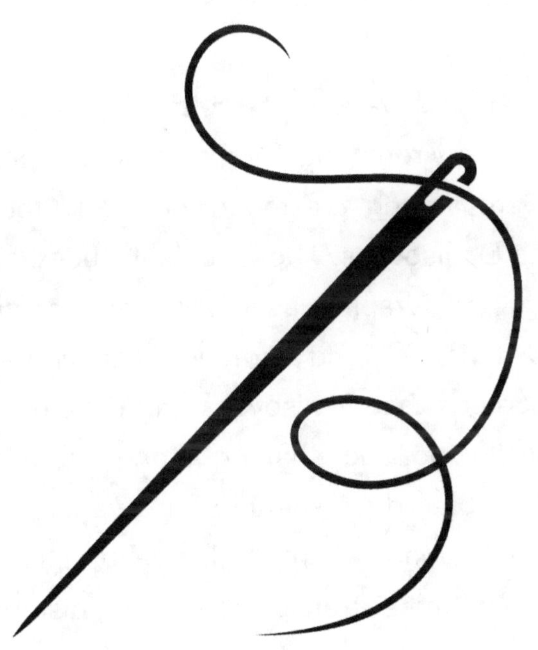

The Denisovans demonstrated remarkable adaptability and ingenuity in their tool-making abilities. Despite the limited archaeological evidence, the tools found in Denisovan sites offer valuable insights into their technological advancements and how these innovations contributed to their survival in diverse and often harsh environments. Their ability to create a wide variety of tools using different materials highlights their sophisticated understanding of tool production and usage, reflecting a complex and intelligent society capable of adapting to various ecological challenges.

Types of Tools and Materials:

Denisovans crafted a variety of tools using materials readily available in their environment, such as stone, bone, and wood. Stone tools were among the most commonly found artifacts associated with Denisovans. These tools included simple flakes used for cutting and scraping, as well as more complex bifacial tools such as handaxes and scrapers. The craftsmanship of these tools suggests that Denisovans had developed advanced techniques for flaking and shaping stone, allowing them to create sharp, durable edges suitable for a variety of tasks. The presence of tools made from high-quality stone materials, which were sometimes transported from distant locations, indicates that Denisovans engaged in extensive trade or mobility to acquire the best resources for tool-making. This ability to source and utilize high-quality materials demonstrates a level of planning and foresight indicative of advanced cognitive abilities.

In addition to stone, Denisovans utilized bone and antler to create tools. These materials were used to fashion needles, awls, and other implements essential for tasks such as sewing clothing and processing hides. The use of bone and antler required different techniques from stone working, showcasing the Denisovans' versatility and innovation in exploiting various resources. Bone tools were particularly useful for creating finer, more delicate implements that stone could not easily produce. This ability to work with multiple materials and create specialized tools reflects a high degree of technological sophistication and adaptability to different environmental challenges. Notably, the discovery of a bone needle is remarkable within this series, highlighting an advanced level of craftsmanship and an innovative approach to creating tools necessary for making clothing, which was crucial for survival in colder climates.

While wooden tools are less likely to survive in the archaeological record due to their perishable nature, it is likely that Denisovans also employed wood for various purposes. Wooden spears and digging sticks would have been essential for hunting and gathering, complementing their stone and bone tools. The use of wood would have provided additional flexibility and utility, particularly in environments where stone resources were scarce. The ability to craft and use wooden tools indicates a broad understanding of available resources and the skills needed to exploit them effectively.

Tool-Making Techniques:

The techniques used by Denisovans in tool-making were sophisticated and varied, reflecting their adaptation to different environmental challenges. The process of knapping, or shaping stone by striking it with another hard object, was a fundamental technique in Denisovan tool-making. This method allowed them to produce sharp-edged tools by carefully removing flakes from a stone core. Advanced knapping techniques, such as bifacial flaking, enabled Denisovans to create more refined and efficient tools. The precision and skill involved in knapping indicate a deep understanding of stone properties and the ability to control the flaking process to achieve desired shapes and edges.

For tools made from bone and antler, Denisovans employed grinding and polishing techniques to achieve the desired shape and smoothness. These methods were crucial for producing tools that required precise edges and surfaces, such as needles and awls. Grinding and polishing also enhanced the durability and functionality of these tools. The ability to refine and perfect their tools through such techniques highlights the Denisovans' meticulous approach to tool-making and their commitment to creating high-quality implements.

There is evidence to suggest that Denisovans created composite tools, combining different materials to enhance their utility. For example, a spear might have a wooden shaft with a stone or bone tip, secured with plant fibers or animal sinew. This technique was also observed in Homo heidelbergensis, as discussed in the previous book. This innovation allowed Denisovans to optimize the strengths of various materials, creating tools that were both effective and versatile. The creation of composite tools indicates a sophisticated understanding of material properties and the ability to engineer solutions that leveraged the best attributes of each component.

Hunting Tools:

Denisovans created and utilized a variety of sophisticated hunting tools essential for their survival. Stone-tipped spears were particularly integral for hunting large game animals such as mammoths, bison, and reindeer. These tools were meticulously crafted, allowing Denisovans to deliver powerful and precise blows to their prey. The use of spears required the production of sharp, durable tips and the construction of strong, balanced shafts, often made from wood. Additionally, they utilized stone knives or blades, which were essential for butchering and processing game after a successful hunt. These blades, crafted with fine edges, were adept at cutting through tough hides and muscles, enabling the efficient extraction of meat and other valuable resources.

The effectiveness of these hunting tools suggests a high level of skill and coordination among Denisovans, essential for securing sufficient food in their challenging environments. Successful hunting expeditions required strategic planning, extensive knowledge of animal behavior, and cooperation among group members. The social complexity implied by these coordinated efforts highlights the advanced cognitive and social abilities of Denisovan groups. These tools were not just practical; they also facilitated the social sharing of food, reinforcing group bonds and ensuring collective survival. The creation and use of such diverse and effective tools underscore their adaptability and resourcefulness, allowing them to thrive in various harsh environments. Moreover, the ability to innovate and improve their hunting strategies over time likely contributed to their success and resilience as a species.

Creating Clothing:

Bone needles and awls were vital for sewing animal hides into clothing, which provided necessary protection against harsh weather conditions. The creation of such intricate tools from bone showcases the advanced level of Denisovan craftsmanship and their ability to adapt to their environment. Notably, the Denisovans are the first hominin in our series to create sewn clothing. While Homo heidelbergensis wore animal hides, the act of sewing clothes is a significant advancement. This innovation highlights the technological leap and the importance of clothing for survival in colder climates. These tools enabled Denisovans to stitch together hides, creating garments that offered insulation and protection from the elements. This ability to produce functional and possibly tailored clothing indicates a deep understanding of materials and techniques, further reflecting their adaptability and ingenuity. The progression from using hides to sewing clothes shows that as we move through this series, we see increasing sophistication in tool use and behaviors, bringing us closer to modern human technological practices.

Shelters and Their Construction:

Denisovans demonstrated advanced knowledge in constructing shelters that provided protection against harsh weather conditions. The Denisova Cave itself, with its strategic location and natural insulation, served as an ideal habitation site. Archaeological evidence suggests that Denisovans also built temporary shelters using materials such as wood, bone, and animal hides. These structures would have been essential for maintaining warmth and safety, particularly during colder months. The construction of these shelters indicates a high level of ingenuity and adaptability, as Denisovans would have needed to understand and utilize the materials available in their environment effectively. The ability to create stable and insulated living spaces highlights the Denisovans' resourcefulness and technical skills, ensuring their survival in various climatic conditions.

Control of Fire:

Evidence of Denisovan use of fire has been found in the Denisova Cave, suggesting that they had mastered the ability to control fire, which was crucial for survival. Fire would have provided warmth in cold climates, protection from predators, and a means to cook food, making it more digestible and nutritious. The use of fire also facilitated the development of more complex tool-making techniques, such as heat-treating stones to make them easier to flake. This capability is comparable to that of Homo heidelbergensis, indicating that both species had a similar level of mastery over fire. However, the specifics of how Denisovans used and controlled fire, and whether their techniques differed significantly from those of Homo heidelbergensis, remain areas for further research.

Technological and Cultural Implications:

The technological innovations of Denisovans not only highlight their practical abilities but also provide insights into their cultural and cognitive development. The complexity and variety of their tools suggest a high level of intelligence and social organization. Tool-making would have required knowledge transmission and skill development, likely facilitated through teaching and learning within their communities. This cultural transmission of knowledge underscores the sophistication of Denisovan society and their ability to adapt and thrive in a wide range of environments. The presence of specialized tools and the organization of living spaces within sites like the Denisova Cave indicate a well-structured social system that supported the development and use of advanced technologies.

By integrating these insights, we can better appreciate the depth of Denisovan social structures and their advanced tool-making abilities, which played a crucial role in their adaptation and survival across various challenging environments. Understanding these aspects of Denisovan life not only enriches our knowledge of this enigmatic group but also sheds light on the broader patterns of human technological and cultural evolution. The Denisovans' technological innovations reflect a high degree of cognitive complexity and social cooperation, essential elements that contributed to their success as a species in diverse and often harsh environments.

CHAPTER 5:
SOCIAL STRUCTURE AND BEHAVIOR

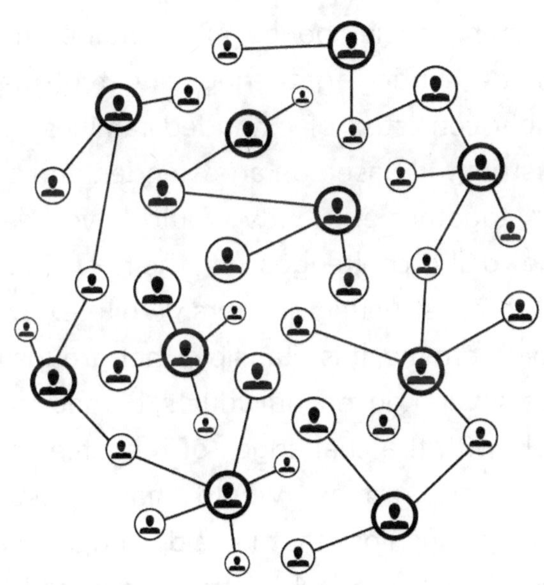

The social structure and behavior of the Denisovans remain largely speculative due to the limited archaeological evidence available. However, what has been uncovered provides intriguing glimpses into their complex social dynamics and cultural practices. By examining the artifacts and environmental contexts of Denisovan sites, particularly the Denisova Cave, we can infer certain aspects of their social organization, community interactions, and behavioral patterns.

Group Size and Composition:

Denisovan social organization likely revolved around small, cohesive groups that relied heavily on cooperation for survival. The harsh and varied environments they inhabited would have necessitated strong social bonds and collaborative efforts in activities such as hunting, gathering, and tool-making. These groups probably consisted of extended families or clans, with social roles distributed based on age, gender, and skill sets. The ability to work together efficiently would have been crucial for managing the daily challenges of their environment, from securing food to constructing shelters. While exact group sizes are difficult to determine, it is plausible that groups ranged from a few dozen to several dozen individuals, balancing the need for mutual support with the challenges of resource scarcity. Living in such close-knit groups would have fostered strong interpersonal relationships, mutual aid, and a deep sense of community. Each group would have likely had one or two leaders, similar to packs of wild animals, who would guide and make crucial decisions for the group. The success of these groups in various harsh environments suggests a well-developed social structure capable of adapting to different ecological challenges.

Care for Group Members:

The harsh environments in which Denisovans lived would have required a strong ethic of care within their communities. Evidence from other archaic human species, such as Neanderthals and Homo heidelbergensis, like we saw in the previous book, suggests that individuals who were injured or ill were cared for by their group members. Similar behavior can be inferred for Denisovans, given the necessity of maintaining the health and well-being of the group to ensure survival. Care for the sick and injured would have included providing food, shelter, and protection, as well as possibly using medicinal plants and other natural remedies. This level of care would have been crucial for the survival of individuals and the group as a whole, reinforcing social bonds and ensuring that everyone contributed to the community's success. The ability to care for one another in times of need would have strengthened social cohesion and trust within the group, essential elements for surviving in challenging environments. Moreover, the shared responsibility of caregiving would have fostered a sense of interdependence and mutual support, further enhancing the resilience and adaptability of Denisovan communities in their diverse and often harsh habitats.

Cooperative Hunting and Resource Sharing:

The cooperative nature of Denisovan society is evident in their hunting strategies and resource-sharing practices. Hunting large game like mammoths and bison required coordinated efforts and sophisticated planning. This level of cooperation indicates a high degree of communication and social cohesion within the group. Once the game was successfully hunted, the butchering and distribution of meat would have been a communal activity, with food shared among all members of the group. This practice not only ensured that everyone had enough to eat but also reinforced social bonds and group cohesion. In addition to hunting, the gathering of plant materials and other resources would have been a communal effort. Knowledge about the locations of edible plants, medicinal herbs, and other useful materials would have been shared among group members, fostering a sense of collective responsibility and interdependence. The division of labor, with specific roles assigned based on individual skills and strengths, would have further enhanced the efficiency and productivity of these communal activities.

Communication and Language:

Effective communication would have been essential for the social cohesion and survival of Denisovan groups. The complexity of their tool-making and social organization suggests that they possessed some form of sophisticated communication, which likely included spoken language, gestures, and possibly symbolic forms of communication. Recent research published in the journal Frontiers in Language Sciences provides strong evidence that modern speech and language existed among Neanderthals, Denisovans, and early Homo sapiens. This evidence, gathered from genetic, fossil, and archaeological studies, indicates that these archaic humans had the basic genetic underpinnings for recognizably modern language and speech. The FOXP2 gene, often linked to language capabilities, is shared between Neanderthals, Denisovans, and modern humans, suggesting that the capacity for language was present in our common ancestor, Homo heidelbergensis. The ability to convey information about hunting strategies, tool-making techniques, and social norms would have been crucial for maintaining group cohesion and transmitting knowledge across generations. The presence of ornamental objects, such as the Denisovan bracelet, hints at symbolic communication and the potential for ritualistic or cultural expression. Advanced communication skills would have been necessary for coordinating group activities, resolving conflicts, and fostering social bonds, all of which were essential for the survival of Denisovan communities in harsh environments. This shared linguistic capability suggests that Denisovans had a high level of cognitive development and social complexity, further underscoring their sophisticated nature.

The genetic similarities between Denisovans, Neanderthals, and modern humans include not only the FOXP2 gene but also other genes involved in brain and nervous system development, supporting the idea that these hominins had the capacity for complex language. Although modern humans might surpass Denisovans in certain aspects of language, such as the range of speech sounds, rapidity of speech, complexity of syntax, and size of vocabularies, the foundational ability for language was likely present in Denisovans. This capacity would have allowed for the development of rich and varied languages, essential for social interaction and cultural transmission. The intricate social structures inferred from their archaeological sites, such as the Denisova Cave, provide further evidence of their sophisticated communication abilities, which would have played a crucial role in their adaptation and survival across diverse environments. By integrating these insights, we can better appreciate the depth of Denisovan social structures and their advanced communication abilities, which played a crucial role in their adaptation and survival across various challenging environments. Understanding these aspects of Denisovan life not only enriches our knowledge of this enigmatic group but also sheds light on the broader patterns of human social evolution.

Learning and Cultural Transmission:

Tool-making was not just a practical skill but also a cultural activity that played a significant role in the social structure of Denisovan communities. The complexity and variety of their tools suggest that knowledge and techniques were passed down through generations, likely through hands-on teaching and learning within the community. This transmission of knowledge would have been crucial for maintaining and improving the technological innovations that were essential for survival. The social aspects of tool-making can be inferred from the presence of specialized tools and the organization of living spaces within sites like the Denisova Cave. Different areas of the cave may have been designated for specific activities, such as tool production, food preparation, and social gatherings. This spatial organization indicates a level of planning and social structure that facilitated the efficient use of space and resources. The production of high-quality tools would have been a valued skill, possibly elevating the social status of skilled toolmakers within the group. The ability to teach and learn complex skills would have been essential for the cultural continuity and advancement of Denisovan society.

Additionally, the Denisovans' ability to innovate and adapt their tools to different environments reflects a dynamic cultural transmission process. This involved not only the replication of existing technologies but also the refinement and adaptation of these technologies to new challenges. Such innovations might have included the development of new hunting tools, methods for processing different types of food, or the creation of more efficient clothing and shelter. The cultural transmission of these innovations would have required a robust system of communication and education within the group, ensuring that each generation could build upon the knowledge and skills of their predecessors. This continuous process of learning and innovation would have been crucial for the survival and success of Denisovan communities, enabling them to thrive in a wide range of environments and adapt to changing conditions over time. The role of elders and experienced individuals in teaching younger members would have been paramount, fostering a deep sense of respect for knowledge and tradition within Denisovan society.

Symbolism, Rituals, and Possible Religion:

Although direct evidence of symbolic behavior among Denisovans is sparse, certain artifacts suggest the presence of ritualistic and symbolic practices. The discovery of a Denisovan bracelet made of chlorite, a relatively rare material, indicates that they created ornamental objects that likely held cultural or symbolic significance. The craftsmanship of this bracelet suggests it was more than a functional item; it may have been used in social or ritual contexts, reflecting the cultural and symbolic aspects of Denisovan life. Rituals and symbolic behavior are important components of social cohesion and cultural identity. Such practices would have helped reinforce group solidarity, transmit cultural values, and navigate social relationships. While the specific nature of Denisovan rituals remains unknown, the presence of ornamental objects and the organization of their living spaces suggest that symbolic behavior was an integral part of their social structure.

There is no direct evidence of religion in Denisovan culture, but the presence of symbolic artifacts hints at the possibility of spiritual or ritualistic beliefs. These practices would have played a crucial role in strengthening social bonds, conveying cultural traditions, and providing a sense of shared identity and purpose within Denisovan communities. The creation of such items and the potential use of ritual spaces would require a significant investment of time and resources, indicating their importance in Denisovan society. However, understanding the full extent of Denisovan symbolic and ritualistic practices remains a challenge due to the limited fossil record. Many aspects of their cultural and spiritual life may never be fully understood without additional discoveries. As such, continued excavation and research are essential to uncover more evidence that could shed light on these intriguing aspects of Denisovan life. All we can do is to wait for more fossil discoveries to provide further insights into their symbolic and ritualistic behaviors.

Art and Cultural Expression:

The Denisovan bracelet is one of the few artifacts that provide a glimpse into their artistic and cultural expression. This artifact demonstrates not only the technical skill required to create such an item but also suggests an appreciation for beauty and possibly status within their society. The creation of ornamental objects indicates that Denisovans engaged in activities beyond mere survival, involving elements of art and personal adornment. This artistic expression would have played a role in social and cultural identity, allowing individuals to display their craftsmanship and possibly signify their status or role within the group.

Recent discoveries have further illuminated the artistic capabilities of the Denisovans. For instance, a 45,000-year-old cave lion figurine made from mammoth ivory was found in the Denisova Cave. This figurine, discovered in the same layers associated with Denisovan occupation, suggests that they engaged in the creation of symbolic and possibly ritualistic art objects. Such artifacts highlight their ability to produce detailed and meaningful art, reflecting both their cognitive abilities and their cultural practices. These artistic endeavors likely played a significant role in social cohesion, conveying cultural traditions, and expressing individual or group identities.

While other examples of Denisovan art have yet to be discovered, the presence of such artifacts suggests a rich cultural life that included artistic and symbolic practices. These practices would have contributed to the cultural richness of Denisovan society, providing a means of expressing individuality, conveying social status, and fostering a sense of community and continuity. The discovery of these art objects underscores the need for more extensive excavations to uncover additional artifacts that can provide further insights into the artistic and cultural expressions of the Denisovans. Such findings would help us understand the full extent of their cultural and artistic heritage, as well as the role these practices played in their daily lives and social structures. As we continue to explore and study Denisovan sites, the potential for new discoveries remains high, offering the promise of deeper insights into the lives of these ancient people.

Adaptation to Environmental Challenges:

The social structure and behavior of Denisovans were undoubtedly shaped by the need to adapt to their diverse and often harsh environments. The ability to cooperate, share resources, and transmit knowledge would have been critical for surviving in regions ranging from the cold, rugged terrains of Siberia to the high-altitude plateaus of Tibet. Social flexibility and the capacity to form strong social bonds would have enabled Denisovan groups to respond effectively to environmental challenges and changes. The Denisova Cave, as a long-term habitation site, provides a unique glimpse into the social and behavioral adaptations of Denisovans. Its strategic location and evidence of repeated use over thousands of years highlight the importance of stable, well-organized social structures in ensuring the survival and success of Denisovan communities. The ability to create and maintain such sites indicates a sophisticated level of social organization and an understanding of the importance of communal living spaces.

In conclusion, while much about Denisovan social structure and behavior remains speculative, the available evidence from sites like the Denisova Cave offers valuable insights into their complex social dynamics. The cooperative nature of their society, their sophisticated tool-making and cultural transmission, and their possible symbolic and ritualistic behaviors all point to a highly organized and adaptive people. Understanding these aspects of Denisovan life not only enriches our knowledge of this enigmatic group but also sheds light on the broader patterns of human social evolution. The study of Denisovan social structures and behaviors provides a window into the intricate and dynamic nature of early human societies, highlighting the importance of cooperation, cultural transmission, and adaptability in the survival and success of our ancient ancestors.

CHAPTER 6:

DENISOVANS AND NEANDERTHALS: INTERBREEDING

Later, following the discovery of the first Denisovan remains in 2008, scientists made a groundbreaking revelation in 2018 with the identification of Denisova 11. This hybrid individual, found in the Denisova Cave in Siberia, had a Neanderthal mother and a Denisovan father. This find significantly advanced our understanding of the interactions between these two archaic human species and underscored the complex genetic and cultural exchanges that occurred between them. The interbreeding between Denisovans and Neanderthals not only provided insights into their close evolutionary relationship but also demonstrated how interconnected the hominin species were during the Pleistocene epoch.

Genetic Evidence and Hybrid Discoveries:

The discovery of Denisova 11 provided direct evidence of interbreeding between Denisovans and Neanderthals. Genetic analysis of her bone fragment revealed that she inherited approximately equal amounts of DNA from both Neanderthals and Denisovans. This interbreeding highlights the frequent and significant interactions between these two groups, which inhabited overlapping regions in Eurasia. The Altai Mountains, where the Denisova Cave is located, served as a crucial meeting point for these hominins, facilitating their interactions and genetic exchanges.

Genetic studies have shown that Denisovans and Neanderthals shared a common ancestor around 400,000 to 500,000 years ago. This close evolutionary relationship is reflected in the genetic similarities and the presence of Neanderthal DNA within the Denisovan genome. The Denisovan father of Denisova 11 also carried some Neanderthal genetic traits, indicating that interbreeding events occurred multiple times over thousands of years. These genetic interminglings enriched the gene pools of both species and provided adaptive advantages, such as high-altitude adaptation traits found in modern Tibetan populations.

Cultural and Technological Exchanges:

 The interbreeding between Denisovans and Neanderthals likely involved not only genetic exchanges but also cultural and technological interactions. Both species exhibited advanced tool-making techniques, which they may have shared and refined through their interactions. The archaeological evidence suggests that both groups utilized sophisticated tools, such as stone flakes and blades, essential for hunting and daily survival. These shared technologies indicate a level of cooperation and knowledge transfer between the two groups, further emphasizing their close connection.

 In addition to tool-making, the shared use of fire, construction of shelters, and possibly symbolic practices would have facilitated their coexistence and cooperation. The Denisova Cave, with its rich archaeological deposits, provides evidence of both Denisovan and Neanderthal occupations, highlighting the shared use of this strategic location. The cultural exchanges between these groups likely included the sharing of hunting strategies and possibly even social and ritual practices, which would have strengthened their interactions and mutual survival strategies.

Physical Appearance and Viability of Hybrids:

The hybrid offspring of Denisovans and Neanderthals, such as Denisova 11, likely exhibited a combination of physical traits from both parent species. Given the robust builds of both Denisovans and Neanderthals, hybrids would have inherited strong, muscular physiques, suited for their demanding environments. These hybrids likely possessed the physical strength and endurance necessary to thrive in the harsh climates they inhabited. The facial features of these hybrids might have included a mix of Neanderthal characteristics, such as prominent brow ridges, wide nasal apertures, and elongated skulls, alongside Denisovan traits that remain less well-defined due to the limited fossil record. Their overall appearance would have been a blend of the distinctive features of both parent species, reflecting the genetic contributions from each. Despite these physical differences, the genetic compatibility between Denisovans and Neanderthals suggests that their hybrid offspring were viable and capable of reproducing. Genetic evidence indicates that the Denisovan father of Denisova 11 also had some Neanderthal ancestry, pointing to multiple generations of interbreeding between these groups. This ongoing genetic exchange over time would have facilitated the mixing of traits and contributed to a diverse gene pool, enhancing the adaptability of both populations.

The successful reproduction of hybrids like Denisova 11 implies that Denisovans and Neanderthals were not separate species in the strictest biological sense but rather distinct populations capable of producing fertile offspring. This genetic exchange contributed to the genetic diversity and adaptability of these hominin groups, enriching their gene pools and providing advantages that enhanced their survival. The viability of these hybrids underscores the fluid boundaries between different hominin groups and highlights the interconnectedness of our evolutionary history. The ability to produce fertile offspring ensured that beneficial genetic traits could be passed down, promoting the survival and success of these populations. This genetic intermingling also allowed for the sharing of advantageous adaptations, such as those related to immune response and environmental resilience, thereby increasing the overall fitness of their descendants. The genetic legacy of these interbreeding events is still evident in modern human populations, particularly in regions where Denisovan and Neanderthal genes have persisted, further illustrating the lasting impact of these ancient interactions on our evolutionary journey.

Implications for Human Evolution:

The interbreeding between Denisovans and Neanderthals has profound implications for our understanding of human evolution. It demonstrates that the boundaries between different hominin species were permeable, with frequent genetic exchanges that shaped the evolutionary trajectories of these groups. This genetic intermingling contributed to the diversity and adaptability of subsequent human populations. For instance, certain Denisovan genes related to immune response and high-altitude adaptation have been identified in modern human populations, particularly in Southeast Asia and the Pacific Islands.

The frequent interbreeding events highlight the adaptability and resilience of these archaic humans, who successfully navigated the challenges of their environments by forming alliances and sharing knowledge and resources. This interconnectedness among hominin species underscores the complexity of human evolution and the collaborative nature of survival during the Pleistocene epoch.

In conclusion, the discovery of Denisova 11 and the genetic evidence of interbreeding between Denisovans and Neanderthals provide a deeper understanding of the close evolutionary and cultural connections between these archaic human species. These interactions not only enriched their gene pools but also facilitated the sharing of knowledge and technologies, contributing to their survival and adaptability. As we continue to uncover more evidence, the intricate web of relationships between hominin species becomes clearer, revealing a dynamic and interconnected history that has shaped the human lineage.

CHAPTER 7:

DENISOVANS AND US: INTERBREEDING

Instead of discovering another fossil evidencing interbreeding, scientists this time compared the DNA of Denisovans to modern humans and found remarkable connections. These interbreeding events, evidenced through genetic analysis, have significantly shaped the genetic makeup of contemporary human populations, particularly in regions such as Southeast Asia and Oceania. The genetic legacy left by Denisovans in these populations underscores the deep connections and interactions between different hominin species throughout our evolutionary history.

Genetic Contributions to Modern Humans:

The genetic contributions of Denisovans to modern human populations are most pronounced in people from Southeast Asia, Melanesia, and the Pacific Islands. Studies have shown that individuals from these regions can have up to 5-6% of their DNA inherited from Denisovans. This genetic inheritance includes genes that have been linked to important adaptations, such as those for high-altitude living in Tibetan populations. The Denisovan variant of the EPAS1 gene, which is involved in oxygen sensing and adaptation to low oxygen levels, has been found in Tibetans, enabling them to thrive in the hypoxic environment of the Tibetan Plateau. This gene is a prime example of how interbreeding with Denisovans provided modern humans with beneficial traits that enhanced their survival in diverse and challenging environments. The extensive presence of Denisovan DNA in these regions highlights the profound impact of these archaic humans on our genetic heritage and underscores the interconnectedness of our evolutionary past.

Health and Immunity:

 Another significant area where Denisovan genes have impacted modern humans is in health and immunity. Some Denisovan genetic variants are associated with enhanced immune responses, which would have conferred advantages in resisting infections and adapting to new pathogens encountered as humans migrated into new territories. These genetic contributions likely played a crucial role in the successful expansion and adaptation of modern human populations across various ecological niches. The presence of these immune-related genes in modern humans illustrates the lasting impact of Denisovan genetics on our ability to withstand diseases and thrive in diverse environments. This genetic legacy underscores the importance of interbreeding in enhancing the resilience and adaptability of human populations throughout history.

Shared Cultural and Technological Practices:

 In addition to genetic contributions, the interbreeding events between Denisovans and modern humans may have also facilitated the exchange of cultural and technological practices. Archaeological evidence suggests that there was a sharing of tool-making techniques and possibly other cultural elements. The use of advanced stone tools, the control of fire, and the construction of shelters are practices that could have been influenced by interactions between Denisovans and early modern humans. These cultural exchanges would have further strengthened the connections between these groups, fostering a sense of shared knowledge and cooperation that contributed to their mutual survival and success. The transfer of these technologies and practices highlights the deep cultural interconnections that shaped the evolutionary trajectories of both Denisovans and modern humans, emphasizing the collaborative nature of their coexistence.

Physical Appearance and Viability of Hybrids:

The hybrid offspring of Denisovans and modern humans likely displayed a fascinating blend of physical characteristics inherited from both parent species. Denisovans, known for their robust skeletal structure, contributed traits that included a larger, more muscular build, well-suited for endurance and strength in harsh environments. Early modern humans, on the other hand, provided a more gracile frame with distinct features such as reduced brow ridges and smaller facial structures compared to their archaic relatives.

Facial features of these hybrids would have been particularly intriguing, combining elements such as the prominent brow ridges and wide nasal apertures of Denisovans with the finer, more delicate features of modern humans. Additionally, Denisovans are thought to have had a wider skull, which would be a notable trait in their hybrid descendants. These individuals likely possessed a diverse array of physical characteristics that enabled them to adapt to various ecological niches and climates, demonstrating the evolutionary advantages of genetic diversity.

The viability of these hybrids was not merely theoretical but evidenced by the genetic contributions found in contemporary human populations. Genetic studies reveal that modern humans, particularly those in Southeast Asia and Oceania, carry a significant proportion of Denisovan DNA. Individuals from Oceania possess the highest percentage of Denisovan ancestry, with up to 5-6% of their genome derived from Denisovans. Southeast Asians and South Asians also exhibit notable Denisovan genetic contributions, although to a lesser extent. In contrast, populations in Europe, Africa, and the Americas have little to no Denisovan DNA.

This successful reproduction and integration of Denisovan-human hybrids highlight the fluidity of species boundaries during the Pleistocene epoch. Rather than existing as isolated groups, Denisovans and early modern humans interacted, interbred, and exchanged beneficial genetic traits. This genetic intermingling fostered a rich tapestry of human diversity, equipping future generations with a broad spectrum of adaptive traits. The ability of hybrids to thrive and reproduce underscores the interconnected nature of human evolution, where the exchange of genetic material across different hominin groups played a crucial role in shaping our species.

Denisovan DNA and Human Genetic Diversity:

Denisovan DNA is found in varying amounts across different continents. Individuals from Oceania, particularly Melanesians and Aboriginal Australians, have the highest percentage of Denisovan ancestry, ranging between 4-6%. Southeast Asians and South Asians also show notable Denisovan genetic contributions, although less than Oceanians. In contrast, Denisovan DNA is nearly absent in European, African, and American populations. This distribution pattern reflects the historical migrations and interbreeding events between early modern humans and Denisovans as they spread across Asia and beyond

Evolutionary Significance:

Denisovans diverged from the common ancestor shared with modern humans and Neanderthals around 600,000 years ago. The genetic difference between Denisovans and modern humans is approximately 2.33%, while Neanderthals differ by about 1.22%, and chimpanzees by about 8.86%. These percentages highlight the evolutionary distances and the shared heritage among these groups. The closer genetic relationship between Denisovans, Neanderthals, and modern humans compared to chimpanzees underscores the complexity and interconnectedness of hominin evolution. The Denisovan contribution to the modern human gene pool demonstrates the adaptive benefits gained through interbreeding, such as enhanced immune responses and physiological adaptations like high-altitude tolerance in certain populations.

Physical Traits and Diversity:

The genetic legacy of Denisovans is also reflected in the physical diversity observed among modern human populations. Certain physical traits, such as robust builds and specific facial features, may have been inherited from Denisovans. This genetic diversity has contributed to the wide range of physical appearances seen in human populations today, highlighting the complex and interconnected nature of human evolution. The blending of Denisovan and modern human traits has enriched the genetic tapestry of humanity, creating a more diverse and adaptable species. The presence of Denisovan genes in modern humans demonstrates the fluidity of species boundaries and the extensive genetic exchange that characterized our evolutionary history, resulting in the rich diversity we observe today.

Implications for Understanding Human Evolution:

The interbreeding between Denisovans and modern humans has profound implications for our understanding of human evolution. It challenges the notion of distinct, isolated species and highlights the fluidity of genetic and cultural boundaries between different hominin groups. This interconnectedness has been a driving force in the evolution of Homo sapiens, enabling the exchange of beneficial traits and knowledge that have enhanced our adaptability and resilience. The study of Denisovan genetics continues to reveal new insights into the evolutionary processes that have shaped modern humans, underscoring the importance of interbreeding in our evolutionary history. This understanding of interbreeding events provides a more comprehensive view of human evolution, emphasizing the collaborative and interconnected nature of our past.

In conclusion, the interbreeding between Denisovans and modern humans has left a lasting legacy on contemporary human populations. The genetic contributions from Denisovans have provided important adaptations that have enhanced our survival and diversity. The cultural and technological exchanges facilitated by these interactions have further enriched our understanding of human evolution, highlighting the interconnected and dynamic nature of our species' history. As research continues to uncover the depths of these connections, we gain a more comprehensive and nuanced view of the evolutionary forces that have shaped the human lineage. The ongoing study of Denisovan genetics and their impact on modern humans continues to shed light on the intricate web of relationships that define our shared history, revealing the profound interconnectedness of all human populations.

CHAPTER 8:

INTERACTIONS WITH OTHER SPECIES

Besides Homo sapiens and Neanderthals, Denisovans likely encountered and interacted with several other hominin species during their existence. Among these, Homo erectus stands out as a significant contemporary. Homo erectus, known for its longevity and wide geographical spread, existed from approximately 1.9 million to 110,000 years ago, overlapping with the Denisovans in time and possibly in space. This species was known for its adaptability and technological advancements, including the use of fire and complex tools. The coexistence of these species suggests potential competition for resources and possibly even the exchange of technological and cultural practices, which could have influenced the evolution and survival strategies of both groups. Homo erectus, with its widespread presence in Asia, Africa, and Europe, would have shared various ecosystems with Denisovans, leading to a dynamic interplay of ecological and social interactions.

Another potential interaction could have been with Homo floresiensis, often referred to as "the Hobbit" due to its small stature. Homo floresiensis lived on the Indonesian island of Flores and existed until about 50,000 years ago. Although direct evidence of interaction between Denisovans and Homo floresiensis is lacking, the geographical proximity suggests the possibility of encounters, particularly given the Denisovans' presence in Asia. The diminutive size of Homo floresiensis and its unique adaptations to island living provide an interesting contrast to the robust and widely dispersed Denisovans, potentially offering insights into how different hominin species adapted to their environments and interacted with one another. The presence of Homo floresiensis in a relatively isolated environment also raises questions about how Denisovans might have navigated and interacted with such distinct populations.

Further, the recently discovered Homo luzonensis, found in the Philippines and dating to around 50,000 years ago, represents another possible hominin Denisovans might have encountered. This diminutive species, characterized by unique dental and skeletal features, adds to the growing complexity of the hominin landscape in Southeast Asia. The existence of multiple hominin species in this region during the late Pleistocene indicates a rich and intricate web of potential interactions, exchanges of technology, culture, and even genetic material. These interactions would have created a dynamic and interconnected landscape of hominin evolution, with each species contributing to the diversity and adaptability of early human populations. Such a mosaic of hominin species highlights the complexity of human evolution and the intricate relationships that shaped our ancestral lineage. The discovery of Homo luzonensis adds another layer to our understanding of human evolution, suggesting that the interactions between different hominin species were far more intricate and widespread than previously thought. This interspecies interaction likely involved competition, cooperation, and possibly even interbreeding, further complicating the evolutionary narrative.

The Denisovan lineages themselves were diverse, with recent DNA analyses revealing at least three distinct groups, including one that might constitute an entirely separate species. This internal diversity among Denisovans indicates a complex evolutionary history and suggests that their interactions with other hominins were varied and multifaceted. These different Denisovan groups might have had unique adaptations and cultural practices, further enriching the tapestry of human evolution during the Pleistocene. For instance, some Denisovan populations, adapted to high-altitude environments, developed unique physiological traits, while others, living in more temperate zones, might have had different sets of survival strategies. The diversity within Denisovan populations reflects a broad range of ecological adaptations and cultural practices, which would have allowed them to thrive in various environments and interact differently with other hominin species. This diversity also implies that Denisovans were not a monolithic group but a collection of populations with distinct evolutionary trajectories, each contributing uniquely to the human story.

Animals They Hunted:

Denisovans lived in diverse environments, from the frigid mountains of Siberia to the tropical forests of Southeast Asia. This variety in habitats meant they hunted a wide range of animals, adapting their strategies and tools to the available fauna. The adaptability of Denisovans to different ecological niches is reflected in their sophisticated tool-making techniques and hunting strategies, which allowed them to thrive in various environments and sustain their populations over extensive periods. Their ability to develop and refine tools suitable for different hunting and foraging activities showcases their innovation and deep understanding of their surroundings.

In the cold, harsh climates of Siberia and the Altai Mountains, Denisovans likely hunted large, Ice Age megafauna. Mammoths, woolly rhinoceroses, and giant deer would have been among the primary targets. Mammoths, for example, were massive creatures, standing up to 14 feet tall and weighing up to 10 tons. These large animals provided not only meat but also hides for clothing and bones for tools. The hunting of such large prey required advanced planning, cooperation, and sophisticated weaponry, such as stone-tipped spears and coordinated group hunting techniques. The social structure and cooperative behavior necessary for hunting large game suggest a complex societal organization among Denisovans, involving roles and strategies that maximized their chances of successful hunts. This type of hunting would also have necessitated knowledge of animal behavior, migration patterns, and effective communication among group members to coordinate attacks.

In the more temperate and tropical regions of Southeast Asia, Denisovans would have encountered a different array of animals. Here, they might have hunted smaller game, such as deer, wild boar, and various bird species. The dense forests and diverse ecosystems of Southeast Asia would have presented unique challenges and opportunities, requiring Denisovans to develop versatile hunting strategies and tools. In addition to hunting, they would have foraged for fruits, nuts, and other plant resources, utilizing their knowledge of the local flora and fauna to sustain their communities. The presence of rivers and coastal areas would have also provided opportunities for fishing and gathering shellfish, further diversifying their diet and demonstrating their adaptability. This adaptability to various environments highlights the Denisovans' resilience and their ability to exploit different food sources, ensuring their survival across a wide range of habitats.

Denisovans likely employed a variety of sophisticated hunting techniques to capture different types of prey. For large animals like mammoths and woolly rhinoceroses, they would have used coordinated group hunting strategies, with multiple individuals working together to drive the animals into traps or ambushes. These large-scale hunts required not only advanced planning and cooperation but also a deep understanding of animal behavior and migration patterns. By using their collective strength and strategic positioning, Denisovans could efficiently take down these massive creatures. Additionally, they might have utilized natural features of the landscape, such as cliffs or ravines, to trap or corner their prey, enhancing their hunting success.

For smaller game, Denisovans might have relied on stealth and patience, using their knowledge of the animals' habits and movements to capture them effectively. This approach would have involved tracking and ambushing animals, utilizing their keen observational skills to predict the movements of their prey. The development of sophisticated tools, such as stone-tipped spears and blades, was crucial for these hunting activities. These tools allowed Denisovans to deliver precise and lethal blows, ensuring a quick kill and minimizing the risk of injury during the hunt.

In addition to these techniques, Denisovans likely used their remarkable endurance to hunt. Persistence hunting, a method where hunters use their stamina to track and exhaust prey over long distances, may have been employed. This technique relies on the hunters' ability to run for extended periods, outlasting the animal until it becomes too tired to continue. This method, combined with their strategic use of the environment and advanced tools, would have made Denisovans highly effective hunters.

The combination of endurance, strategic planning, and advanced tool use enabled Denisovans to process their kills efficiently and make use of every part of the animal. Meat provided essential nutrients, while hides could be used for clothing and shelter, and bones for tools and weapons. This comprehensive utilization of resources reflects their sophisticated understanding of their environment and their ability to adapt and thrive in various ecological niches. The successful integration of these hunting techniques highlights the Denisovans' ingenuity and adaptability, key factors in their survival and evolutionary success.

Animals That Hunted Them:

Denisovans, like other early humans, had to contend with various predators that posed significant threats to their survival. In the cold regions of Siberia, they would have encountered formidable predators such as cave bears, which were larger than modern bears and could weigh up to a ton. These massive bears, with their powerful builds and sharp claws, were apex predators capable of preying on large mammals, including humans. The presence of cave bears necessitated the development of defensive strategies, such as creating fortified shelters and using fire to deter these formidable predators. Saber-toothed cats, another significant threat, were equipped with elongated canine teeth and robust bodies designed for powerful ambush attacks. The ability of these predators to take down large prey meant that Denisovans had to remain vigilant and develop strategies to avoid becoming their next meal.

In addition to these large predators, Denisovans would have had to be wary of wolves and large packs of predatory canines that roamed the Siberian landscape. These social hunters, capable of taking down prey much larger than themselves through coordinated attacks, posed a constant danger. Denisovans likely relied on their advanced tool-making skills to create weapons for defense, such as spears and clubs, which could be used to fend off these threats. Establishing camps in safe locations and using lookout systems to monitor for approaching predators would have been crucial strategies for ensuring their safety.

In the temperate and tropical regions, Denisovans faced threats from large cats like tigers and leopards. These stealthy and powerful predators could ambush and kill their prey with ease, making them a constant danger to early human populations. Tigers, with their immense strength and ability to blend into dense vegetation, were formidable opponents. Leopards, known for their agility and climbing abilities, could strike from above, adding an element of unpredictability to the threat landscape. Crocodiles and large snakes were additional hazards in riverine and coastal areas. These reptiles, with their powerful jaws and stealthy hunting methods, would have posed significant risks to Denisovans living near water sources.

In more temperate regions, large predatory birds, such as the Haast's eagle, which once roamed parts of Asia, could have also posed a threat to young and vulnerable individuals. These birds, with wingspans reaching up to three meters, were capable of powerful aerial assaults, adding another dimension to the predatory challenges faced by Denisovans.

The need to defend against these predators would have driven the development of social cooperation and sophisticated defensive tools, further enhancing the Denisovans' survival capabilities. Their interactions with these predators required constant vigilance and strategic planning, influencing their daily activities and social structures. Group living would have been essential for mutual protection, with designated sentinels and shared responsibilities for maintaining safety. The development of early warning systems, such as lookouts and alarm calls, would have been critical for detecting and responding to threats swiftly.

In summary, Denisovans had to navigate a perilous world filled with various predators, ranging from large mammals and stealthy big cats to dangerous reptiles and even predatory birds. Their ability to develop advanced defensive strategies, sophisticated tools, and cooperative social structures enabled them to mitigate these threats and ensure their survival. These interactions with predators shaped not only their daily lives but also their evolutionary trajectory, highlighting the resilience and adaptability that have been hallmarks of human evolution.

Interactions with Other Animals:

Beyond the animals they hunted and those that hunted them, Denisovans interacted with a variety of other creatures that shared their habitats. In the vast and varied landscapes they inhabited, Denisovans would have encountered many other species, both extant and extinct, that played significant roles in their ecosystems. These interactions were crucial for understanding their environment and adapting their survival strategies.

In the cold regions of Siberia, alongside the large megafauna, Denisovans might have encountered smaller mammals such as woolly hares and arctic foxes. These animals, while not necessarily hunted, would have been part of the broader ecological context in which Denisovans lived. The presence of woolly hares, known for their rapid reproduction and resilience in cold climates, would have provided Denisovans with indicators of seasonal changes and food availability. Arctic foxes, being scavengers, might have competed with Denisovans for food resources, particularly during harsh winters. Observing the behaviors and population dynamics of these smaller mammals could have provided valuable information about the health and changes in the ecosystem, influencing Denisovan strategies for survival, from scavenging opportunities to indicators of environmental changes.

In the temperate forests and grasslands, Denisovans would have lived alongside a myriad of species, including extinct ones like the straight-tusked elephant, which roamed the forests of Europe and Asia. This large herbivore, which could grow up to 13 feet at the shoulder, would have been a significant part of the ecosystem, affecting plant life and providing opportunities for scavenging. The presence of such large herbivores would have shaped the vegetation patterns and landscape structure, indirectly impacting the Denisovans' access to resources. The straight-tusked elephants' feeding habits would have created clearings in the forest, promoting the growth of certain plants and creating new foraging opportunities for Denisovans. Furthermore, the remains of these massive animals, whether from natural deaths or predation by other carnivores, would have provided scavenging opportunities, allowing Denisovans to utilize every part of the carcass for food, tools, and materials.

In the tropical regions of Southeast Asia, Denisovans would have shared their environment with a range of exotic species, many of which are now extinct. These include the stegodon, an ancient relative of elephants, which could reach up to 13 feet in height. The presence of such large herbivores would have shaped the landscape and the availability of resources for Denisovans. Stegodons, with their massive size and feeding habits, would have had a profound impact on the forest structure, creating pathways and clearings that Denisovans could exploit for travel and hunting. Additionally, they would have encountered diverse primates, birds, and reptiles, all contributing to a rich and complex ecosystem. Primates, for instance, would have been important competitors and possibly even prey, while the diverse bird life could have provided both food sources and indicators of environmental changes. Reptiles, including large snakes and crocodiles, would have posed both threats and opportunities, requiring Denisovans to be constantly vigilant and adaptable.

The Denisovans' interactions with these animals would not have been limited to hunting and defense but also included observation and learning from the behaviors of other species. These interactions would have informed their understanding of the environment, influencing their strategies for hunting, foraging, and survival. Observing the habits of prey and predators alike, Denisovans would have developed a deep ecological knowledge that enhanced their adaptability and resilience. By watching how other animals navigated their environment, found food, and avoided predators, Denisovans could adopt and refine their own strategies. This deep ecological awareness would have been crucial for their survival, allowing them to anticipate changes in the environment and adjust their behaviors accordingly. The intricate web of their interactions and their profound impact on the ecosystems they inhabited highlight the Denisovans' crucial role in the prehistoric world. Their enduring legacy offers a window into the resilience, ingenuity, and interconnectedness that have been hallmarks of human evolution.

Overall, the interactions of Denisovans with other hominin species and their diverse hunting and foraging practices paint a picture of a highly adaptable and innovative group. Their ability to navigate and exploit different ecological niches, interact with other hominins, and develop sophisticated tools and strategies underscores their significance in the broader narrative of human evolution. The legacy of Denisovans, preserved in the genetic and archaeological records, continues to provide valuable insights into the complex web of interactions that shaped the development of our species and its remarkable adaptability. The intricate web of their interactions and their profound impact on the ecosystems they inhabited highlight the Denisovans' crucial role in the prehistoric world. Their enduring legacy offers a window into the resilience, ingenuity, and interconnectedness that have been hallmarks of human evolution.

CHAPTER 9:

A STORY: THE MAMMOTH HUNT

Introduction:

This chapter presents a fictional yet realistic story of a day in the life of a Denisovan group living approximately 44,000 years ago near the Denisova Cave in the Altai Mountains of Siberia, Russia. This story aims to provide an immersive experience into the daily routines, challenges, and social interactions of the Denisovans, based on current anthropological and archaeological understanding of their era and lifestyle.

Altai Mountains In Siberia, 42,000 BCE

The icy winds howled outside the entrance of the cave, adding to the sense of isolation that gripped the Denisovan group huddled inside. The cave, nestled in the rugged Altai Mountains of Siberia, was their refuge against the harsh winter. The group, numbering about 32 individuals, had made a home within the spacious, dimly lit interior of the cave. The walls were adorned with simple drawings and carvings, telling stories of past hunts and adventures. In the heart of the cave, three fireplaces flickered, casting dancing shadows on the stone walls and providing much-needed warmth. Around these fireplaces, most of the group gathered, their faces lit by the soft glow. The fires were essential, not just for warmth, but for cooking food and keeping wild animals at bay. The air was thick with the smell of burning wood and cooked meat, mingling with the earthy scent of the cave itself. Among the group was Lizzy, a 17-year-old Denisovan who stood at 5 feet (153 cm) and weighed 128 pounds (58 kg). Despite her young age, Lizzy was known for her strength, calm nature, and many talents. She was always busy, either crafting tools, helping with hunts, or foraging for food. She had a knack for tracking animals and understanding their behavior, which made her an asset during hunting trips. She often helped the children stay warm and occupied, ensuring they were safe and cared for.

Each member of the group had their own responsibilities and roles, crucial for their survival in the unforgiving environment. The elders, with their vast knowledge and experience, often advised the younger members on hunting, foraging, and crafting tools. Skilled hunters and gatherers secured food, while others focused on maintaining the fires and repairing tools and shelters. Some specialized in using medicinal herbs, tending to the sick and injured. Lizzy's role within the group was varied. Her talents spanned many skills, from crafting intricate tools to assisting in hunts and foraging expeditions. She had a natural ability to understand animal behavior, making her an excellent tracker. Her calm demeanor made her a reliable presence during crises, often stepping in to mediate disputes or provide comfort. As she moved through the cave, she checked on the children, ensuring they were warm and occupied, and offered help to those preparing food or tending the fires. The sense of community was strong among the Denisovans, each person's contribution vital to their collective well-being. As the winter winds battered the world outside, inside the cave, there was a sense of unity and resilience. The group's ability to adapt and work together was their greatest strength, allowing them to endure the long, harsh winters and emerge stronger with each passing season.

Chapter 2: The Hunt Begins:

The food supplies were running low, and the biting cold was growing more intense each day. The group's leader, a seasoned hunter named Torak, decided it was time for a major hunting trip. The goal was to bring down a mammoth, a creature so large that a single one could weigh up to 10 tons. Such a beast would provide more than enough meat to feed the entire group for weeks, along with valuable hides and bones for clothing, shelter, and tools. As the decision was made, a flurry of activity erupted in the cave. Everyone began to prepare their gear, checking and rechecking their tools and weapons. Lizzy, with a determined smile, joined in. She grabbed some old mammoth meat that had been hunted months ago and preserved by the cold, which prevented it from rotting. This would serve as her food for the journey. She also gathered her hunting tools: a stone knife, carefully crafted for skinning and cutting meat, and three very sharp wooden spears she had made herself. These spears, with their finely honed tips, were designed for both throwing and thrusting, making them versatile weapons for the hunt. Lizzy's hands moved swiftly and confidently, her breath visible in the frigid air as she ensured everything was in place. The anticipation of the hunt filled her with a mixture of excitement and purpose.

By 7 AM, twelve hunters, including Lizzy, were ready to depart. They were a formidable group, each one skilled and experienced in the ways of the hunt. The cold air bit at their faces as they stepped out of the warmth of the cave, but their spirits were high. They knew that this hunt was crucial for their survival, and they were prepared to face whatever challenges lay ahead. As they trudged through the snow, the landscape around them was stark and silent, the trees heavy with frost. The group moved with practiced ease, each step deliberate and coordinated. Lizzy felt a sense of anticipation and focus, her senses sharpened by the cold and the purpose of the hunt. She exchanged glances with her fellow hunters, their expressions mirroring her own determination. The journey to the hunting grounds was long and arduous. They had to traverse icy streams, climb steep hills, and navigate dense forests. Each step required caution and strength, as the frozen ground and hidden patches of ice posed constant threats. The hunters communicated in hushed tones and some words, sharing observations and plans. Along the way, they remained vigilant, scanning the terrain for any signs of their prey. Tracks, broken branches, and trampled snow told them that mammoths had recently passed through the area. The excitement among the group grew as they realized they were getting closer to their target. Finally, they started to walk faster, the vast expanse of snowy wilderness stretching out before them as they embarked on their crucial mission.

Chapter 3: The Hunt Begins:

On their way to the hunting grounds, the group decided to take a short break as they knew they were getting close to their target. They sat down, ate some of the old mammoth meat they had brought with them, and drank water from their leather flasks. Lizzy laid down in a field of grass and flowers, enjoying the brief respite. She always liked these hunting trips, not just for the thrill of the chase but also for the beauty of the unknown. The cold air was refreshing, and the sight of the clear sky above made her feel alive and ready for the hunt. The momentary peace and the gentle rustling of the grass and flowers around her allowed her a brief escape from the harsh realities of their daily struggle for survival.

After the break, the group continued their journey and soon spotted a pack of mammoths grazing in the distance. The massive creatures were tearing at the sparse vegetation, their thick fur coats moving slightly in the wind. The leader, Torak, quickly formulated a plan. They decided to split into two groups. Eight of them, including Torak, would start the hunt by chasing the mammoths, trying to separate one from the pack. The other four hunters, including Lizzy, would move ahead to the direction where the chase would likely lead, finding some kind of cover to ambush the mammoths as they ran past. This strategy required precise timing and coordination, with each group playing a crucial role in ensuring the success of the hunt.

 The four hunters chosen for the ambush set off first, moving quickly and quietly through the snow. Lizzy, along with the three others, searched for a suitable spot where they could hide and wait for the mammoths to be driven toward them. They needed a place that offered good cover but also a clear view of the approaching herd. They found a dense cluster of trees and bushes, providing the perfect vantage point. They crouched down, spears at the ready, hearts pounding in anticipation. Meanwhile, the main group of eight stayed behind, watching and waiting. Lizzy felt the tension building as they waited for the signal from Torak. They had no way of knowing if the ambushers had found a good hiding spot or not, but they trusted in their skill and experience. The weight of responsibility hung heavy on Lizzy, but she steeled herself, ready to act when the moment came.

 About twenty minutes later, the main group was still waiting in silence. The cold air felt sharper, and every second seemed to stretch on forever. Then, without warning, Torak gave the signal. He had judged the moment was right. The hunters sprang into action, their coordinated movements breaking the stillness of the morning. They began to chase the mammoths, shouting and waving their spears to drive the massive beasts into a panic. Lizzy, from her hidden position, could hear the distant roars and the thunderous stomping of the mammoths as they were driven towards her.

The only sound that followed was the thunderous noise of mammoths running in all directions, their heavy footsteps shaking the ground. The main group continued their pursuit, driving the herd toward the ambushers. Lizzy tightened her grip on her spear, muscles tensed, eyes fixed on the approaching behemoths. The plan was set into motion, and all they could do now was trust that their fellow hunters were in place and ready to strike. The sight of the mammoths growing larger as they barreled closer made Lizzy's heart race, knowing that soon, their skills and bravery would be put to the ultimate test.

Chapter 4: The Hunt Intensifies

The mammoth was chosen—a colossal beast weighing 6 tons of meat and muscle. As the hunters closed in, they launched their spears with precision. Four spears struck the mammoth: three embedded in its back and one in its leg. Hitting this massive creature was no easy feat, as mammoths could run up to 40 kilometers per hour. Despite the injuries, the mammoth continued its desperate run. Torak, with his keen aim, landed the fifth spear, yet the mammoth pressed on, its sheer will driving it forward.

The mammoth barreled through a cluster of trees, its enormous form crashing through the underbrush. It continued to run for another five minutes before finally stopping to catch its breath. Although its speed could outpace most humans, its massive size worked against its endurance. For a brief moment, all was calm. The heavy breathing of the mammoth filled the air as it stood still, muscles quivering with exhaustion.

From the cover of the trees, two hunters emerged: Lizzy and a fellow hunter named Debra. With practiced precision, they launched their spears, each embedding two into the mammoth's left leg. The beast roared in pain, its leg buckling under the assault. Following swiftly, the other two hunters appeared and drove their spears into its back. The mammoth, fueled by pain and fear, started running again.

Lizzy and Debra were relentless. They chased the mammoth, their eyes fixed on the towering creature as it lumbered away. The other two hunters broke off, heading back to find the main group and lead them to the fleeing mammoth. Despite its injuries, the mammoth's speed once again allowed it to outdistance the humans. It took another brief respite, but as it turned, it saw Lizzy and Debra closing in. With a desperate surge of energy, it began to run again.

This harrowing chase repeated itself three more times. Each time, the mammoth would outrun the hunters and take a moment to recover, only to see Lizzy and Debra drawing near once more. The relentless pursuit wore on the mammoth, its strength waning with each burst of effort. By the fourth time, the injuries and exhaustion took their toll. The mammoth could run no more. It stood still, sides heaving, blood seeping from its wounds, eyes wide with a mixture of fear and anger.

As Lizzy and Debra approached, the mammoth let out a thunderous bellow. The sound echoed through the forest, a mix of rage and desperation. The two hunters steeled themselves, their own adrenaline surging. The mammoth's primal scream was met with their own battle cries as they prepared for the final confrontation. Both sides, driven by the instinct to survive, charged at each other. The mammoth, despite its injuries, lowered its head, ready to fight. Lizzy and Debra, with spears poised, ran towards the massive creature. And with both fear and anger, all three creatures screamed in their own way and headed toward each other with the instinct to kill.

Chapter 5: The Final Stand:

Five meters before the clash, Lizzy made a quick decision and veered sharply to the right. Debra mirrored her move, darting to the left. Both hunters, in perfect synchrony, hurled their spears at the mammoth's back legs. The mammoth let out a piercing scream, its massive body trembling with pain. Lizzy, now out of spears, quickly grabbed her knife and stood ready, watching the mammoth's reaction. Debra, with her last spear in hand, approached the mammoth cautiously and thrust it into its chest. Instead of succumbing, the mammoth roared in fury. It stood tall and began to charge directly at Lizzy and Debra.

Both hunters turned and ran, heading back toward the place they had started the chase, hoping to meet up with the other ten hunters. Their hearts pounded as they sprinted through the snow, the mammoth's heavy footsteps thundering behind them. Just as they had hoped, they reunited with the rest of the group. Torak, however, signaled for them to hold their attack. The mammoth's speed was beginning to falter, its strength waning with each passing moment.

Torak approached Lizzy and Debra, his eyes filled with determination. He explained that the closer they could lead the mammoth to the cave, the easier it would be to transport the meat back. With renewed resolve, the group resumed the chase, steering the mammoth back along the path they had come. The massive beast, driven by pain and exhaustion, could only manage a slow, stumbling run. It wasn't long before its strength gave out completely. With a final, shuddering breath, the mammoth collapsed to the ground, accepting its fate. It closed its eyes and never opened them again.

Their hunt had been successful, and even more fortunate was the fact that the mammoth had fallen close to the cave. Two hunters immediately set off to the cave to bring additional help for butchering and transporting the meat before nightfall. The remaining hunters began the initial preparations, their hands working swiftly and efficiently. Lizzy, her body aching from the exertion, found a nearby rock and sat down. She drank deeply from her water flask, the cool liquid soothing her dry throat. As she looked up at the sky, a sense of profound satisfaction washed over her.

The sky was beginning to shift from the pale light of day to the deep hues of evening. The success of their hunt meant survival for their group, and the proximity of the kill to their cave made the task of bringing back the meat significantly easier. As she sat there, watching the sky, Lizzy felt a deep connection to her ancestors and the land they called home. The hunt had tested their strength, skill, and endurance, but it had also reinforced the bonds between them.

As the additional hunters arrived from the cave, the group worked together to carve up the mammoth. The task was immense, but their combined efforts made it manageable. They worked with a sense of urgency, knowing that the night would bring even colder temperatures. Despite the physical exhaustion, there was an air of triumph and camaraderie among them. Lizzy, now fully rested, joined in the efforts, her hands steady and sure as she helped with the butchering.

By the time the last light of day faded from the sky, the hunters had managed to process most of the mammoth. They carried the precious meat, hides, and bones back to the cave, their steps lighter with the knowledge of a successful hunt. Inside the cave, fires were stoked, and the scent of cooking meat filled the air. The group gathered around the warmth, sharing stories of the hunt and celebrating their victory.

Lizzy sat near the fire, her body tired but her spirit invigorated. She knew that this hunt was not just about survival but also about the strength and unity of their group. They had faced the challenges together, and together they had succeeded. As she looked at the faces of her companions, illuminated by the flickering firelight, she felt a deep sense of pride and belonging. The stars began to appear in the night sky, a silent witness to their resilience and determination.

CHAPTER 10:
ROLE IN HUMAN EVOLUTION

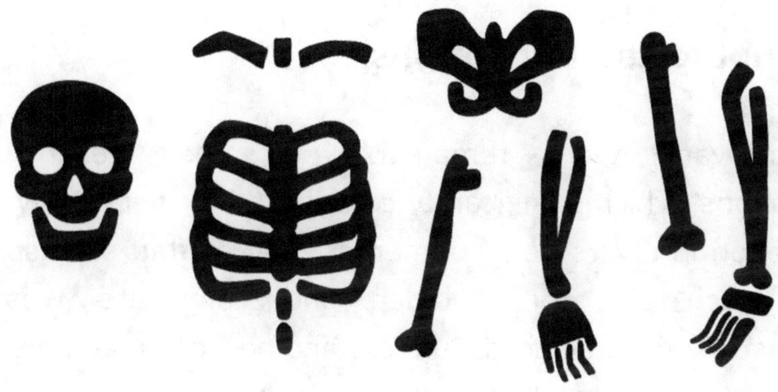

The Denisovans, an enigmatic group of archaic humans, have left an indelible mark on the story of human evolution. Through their technological innovations, extensive geographic dispersal, unique biological adaptations, and complex social structures, Denisovans contributed significantly to the development of early human societies. Their interactions with other hominins, as well as their ability to adapt and thrive in diverse environments, highlight their importance in understanding our own evolutionary journey. This chapter delves into various aspects of Denisovan life and their role in human evolution, providing a comprehensive overview of their impact and legacy. By examining their technological advancements, geographic spread, anatomical changes, and social behaviors, we can gain deeper insights into how the Denisovans shaped the course of human history.

Technological Innovations:

Denisovans were remarkable for their technological innovations, which significantly contributed to their survival and adaptation in diverse environments. They crafted sophisticated tools, such as stone blades and composite weapons, demonstrating advanced understanding of materials and mechanics. Their toolkits included finely worked stone tools, bone needles for sewing, and evidence of possibly creating ornamental objects like bracelets. These tools were not only functional but also indicated a level of cognitive development that allowed for the planning and execution of complex tasks. The Denisovans' ability to innovate and refine their technology showcases their resourcefulness and adaptability, enabling them to thrive in harsh and varied climates. Their technological prowess, passed down through generations, played a crucial role in their ability to hunt, gather, and protect themselves from predators, underscoring their significant contributions to early human technological progress. This innovation extended to their construction of shelters and clothing, which were essential for survival in extreme climates, highlighting their ingenuity and problem-solving skills. The Denisovans' mastery of tool-making and use of advanced techniques reflect a sophisticated understanding of their environment and their ability to manipulate it to their advantage.

Geographic Dispersal and Adaptation:

The Denisovans exhibited a remarkable geographic dispersal, spreading across vast regions from Siberia to Southeast Asia. This wide range of habitats required them to adapt to diverse climates and ecosystems, from the frigid, mountainous terrains of Siberia to the tropical forests of Southeast Asia. Their ability to survive and thrive in these varied environments is a testament to their adaptability and resilience. Evidence of Denisovan genetic markers in modern populations across Asia and Oceania indicates their extensive migration and interaction with other hominin groups. This dispersal not only highlights their adaptability but also their role in the broader narrative of human migration and evolution. The Denisovans' capacity to adapt to different ecological niches underscores their evolutionary success and their integral part in the human story. Their presence in such diverse regions suggests a high degree of mobility and sophisticated survival strategies, enabling them to exploit a variety of resources and establish communities in different environments. The Denisovans' ability to adapt to different climatic conditions and geographic landscapes highlights their versatility and resilience, ensuring their survival over millennia.

Biological and Anatomical Changes:

Biological and anatomical changes in Denisovans reflect their adaptations to their environment and their evolutionary journey. They possessed robust builds, likely an adaptation to cold climates, with large, strong bones and powerful muscles. Their physical strength would have been crucial for hunting large prey and surviving in harsh conditions. Additionally, Denisovans had unique dental and skeletal features, such as their large molars and distinctive dental arch, which set them apart from other hominins. These anatomical differences provide insights into their diet and lifestyle, suggesting a high-protein diet possibly rich in meat. The Denisovans' biological adaptations highlight their ability to survive and thrive in diverse environments, contributing to their longevity and evolutionary significance. Their physical attributes not only aided in their survival but also in their social and cultural practices, influencing their daily activities and interactions within their groups. The Denisovans' unique anatomical features, such as their robust skeletal structure and large molars, reflect their evolutionary adaptations to their specific environments and dietary needs, showcasing their ability to thrive under diverse and challenging conditions.

Brain Size and Intelligence:

Denisovans had brain sizes comparable to modern humans, suggesting a high level of intelligence. This is evident from their sophisticated tool-making abilities and the possible creation of symbolic objects. Their cognitive capabilities would have enabled them to plan complex hunting strategies, communicate effectively within their groups, and adapt to changing environments. The presence of advanced tools and evidence of possible cultural practices indicate that Denisovans had developed significant intellectual abilities. Their brain size and associated cognitive functions underscore their role in the broader human evolutionary narrative, highlighting their contributions to the development of human intelligence and culture. The intellectual achievements of the Denisovans are further evidenced by their ability to innovate and adapt, showcasing their significant cognitive capabilities and their contributions to early human society. Their ability to create and use complex tools, plan sophisticated hunting strategies, and engage in symbolic behavior highlights their advanced cognitive functions and their role in the evolution of human intelligence.

Social Structure and Behavior:

The social structure and behavior of Denisovans were likely complex and cooperative, crucial for their survival in harsh environments. They lived in small, cohesive groups, with social roles distributed based on age, gender, and skills. Cooperative hunting, food sharing, and mutual care within the group would have been essential for maintaining group cohesion and survival. Evidence of sophisticated tool use and potential symbolic artifacts suggests a rich social and cultural life. The Denisovans' social behaviors, including their ability to work together and support each other, reflect their advanced social structures and their significant role in the development of early human societies. Their social organization would have included the division of labor and the transmission of knowledge across generations, reinforcing the importance of community and cooperation in their survival. The intricate social structures of the Denisovans, including their cooperative hunting strategies, food sharing practices, and care for the sick and injured, underscore their sophisticated social organization and their ability to maintain cohesive and supportive communities.

Interbreeding and Genetic Legacy:

 Denisovans' interbreeding with other hominin groups, such as Neanderthals and early modern humans, left a lasting genetic legacy. Genetic studies have revealed Denisovan DNA in modern human populations, particularly in Asia and Oceania, indicating significant interbreeding events. This genetic mixing contributed to the genetic diversity and adaptability of modern humans. Traits inherited from Denisovans, such as those related to immune response and adaptation to high altitudes, highlight their impact on human evolution. The Denisovans' interbreeding with other hominins underscores their role in shaping the genetic makeup of contemporary human populations and their importance in the broader narrative of human evolution. This genetic legacy continues to influence human biology today, reflecting the deep and lasting impact of Denisovan interbreeding on our species. The Denisovans' genetic contributions to modern human populations, including traits for immune response and high-altitude adaptation, underscore their significant and lasting impact on human evolution and highlight the interconnectedness of different hominin groups in our evolutionary history.

Cultural and Cognitive Contributions:

 The cultural and cognitive contributions of Denisovans are evident in their sophisticated tool-making and potential symbolic practices. Artifacts such as the Denisovan bracelet suggest a level of cultural and artistic expression, indicating cognitive abilities similar to those of other contemporary hominins. These contributions reflect their capacity for abstract thinking, planning, and cultural development. The presence of advanced tools and potential symbolic artifacts highlights the Denisovans' role in the development of early human culture and cognition. Their contributions to cultural and cognitive evolution are significant, showcasing their place in the broader human story. The ability to create symbolic objects and engage in complex cultural practices demonstrates their advanced cognitive abilities and their influence on the development of human culture. The Denisovans' cultural and cognitive contributions, including their ability to create intricate tools and engage in symbolic behavior, highlight their advanced cognitive functions and their role in shaping early human culture and societal development.

Hunting Huge Preys:

 Denisovans were adept hunters, capable of taking down large prey such as mammoths and woolly rhinoceroses. Their hunting strategies likely involved coordinated group efforts, sophisticated tools, and deep knowledge of animal behavior. The ability to hunt large animals provided them with substantial food resources, essential for their survival in harsh environments. This skill not only reflects their physical strength and technological capabilities but also their social cooperation and planning abilities. The successful hunting of large prey underscores the Denisovans' adaptability and resourcefulness, highlighting their crucial role in early human survival and evolution. Their prowess in hunting large animals underscores their importance in the prehistoric ecosystem and their significant contributions to human evolutionary success. The

Denisovans' advanced hunting strategies, involving coordinated group efforts and sophisticated tools, highlight their physical strength, technological capabilities, and social cooperation, showcasing their essential role in early human survival and evolutionary success.

In summary, the Denisovans played a vital role in the tapestry of human evolution. Their technological innovations, wide geographic dispersal, unique biological traits, and complex social structures have left an enduring legacy that continues to shape our understanding of early human history. Through interbreeding, they have contributed to the genetic diversity of modern populations, and their cognitive and cultural contributions have enriched the story of human development. The Denisovans' ability to adapt and thrive in diverse environments, coupled with their advanced hunting strategies, underscores their significance in the broader narrative of human evolution. As we continue to uncover more about their lives and interactions, the Denisovans remain a key piece in the puzzle of our shared ancestry, illustrating the intricate and interconnected nature of human history. The lasting impact of the Denisovans on modern human populations and their contributions to technological, social, and cultural developments highlight their essential role in the broader narrative of human evolution, emphasizing their enduring significance and the interconnectedness of our shared human journey.

CHAPTER II:
HOW THEY BECAME EXTINCT

The extinction of the Denisovans remains one of the great mysteries of human evolution. Their disappearance, like that of many other archaic human species, is a complex interplay of environmental, biological, and social factors. Around 40,000 years ago, the world was undergoing significant climatic changes, with the end of the last Ice Age bringing about dramatic shifts in habitats and resources. These environmental changes would have put immense pressure on Denisovan populations, challenging their ability to find food and maintain their communities. The dramatic alterations in climate led to the transformation of ecosystems, affecting the availability of plants and animals that Denisovans had relied on for millennia. The resulting scarcity of resources likely triggered a survival crisis for Denisovans, forcing them to adapt rapidly or face the dire consequences of starvation and displacement.

As the climate warmed, the habitats that Denisovans had adapted to for thousands of years began to change. Forests and grasslands transformed, altering the availability of plants and animals that Denisovans relied on for sustenance. This shift in ecosystems likely forced Denisovans to compete with other species, including modern humans and Neanderthals, for dwindling resources. Competition for food and territory may have led to conflicts, further stressing Denisovan populations. The presence of other human species, each vying for the same resources, intensified the struggle for survival. These interactions, often hostile, would have drained the energy and resources of Denisovan groups, weakening their capacity to thrive.

The arrival of Homo sapiens into Denisovan territories might have also played a crucial role in their extinction. Modern humans brought advanced tools, complex social structures, and perhaps new diseases to which Denisovans had no immunity. The superior technology and social organization of Homo sapiens could have given them an edge in survival, pushing Denisovans to the brink. Interbreeding between Denisovans and modern humans, while enriching the genetic pool, may have also diluted distinct Denisovan lineages over time. The influx of Homo sapiens likely introduced new survival strategies and competitive pressures that Denisovans were unprepared for, accelerating their decline. The blending of populations through interbreeding, while beneficial in some respects, also led to the gradual disappearance of pure Denisovan lineages, making it difficult for them to maintain their unique identity.

Moreover, genetic evidence suggests that Denisovans interbred with Neanderthals and early modern humans. While this interbreeding contributed to the genetic diversity of contemporary human populations, it may have also played a role in their eventual absorption into larger, more dominant groups. The Denisovan genetic legacy lives on in modern humans, particularly in populations in Asia and Oceania, indicating that their genes were absorbed into our lineage rather than being entirely lost. This interbreeding, while enriching the genetic tapestry of modern humans, also meant that Denisovans as a distinct group slowly disappeared, their genetic traits merging with those of other human populations. The blending of these lineages underscores the interconnectedness of human evolution and the fluid boundaries between different human species.

The most popular theories on how Denisovans became extinct revolve around the impact of climate change and competition with modern humans. The end of the last Ice Age brought significant environmental changes, which would have drastically altered the habitats and food sources available to Denisovans. As forests and grasslands transformed, Denisovans faced increasing pressure to adapt to new conditions. Simultaneously, the arrival of Homo sapiens, equipped with advanced technology and social structures, introduced new competition. Modern humans' superior hunting tools, organizational skills, and perhaps even new diseases could have created insurmountable challenges for Denisovan populations. The combined effects of environmental stress and competitive disadvantages likely led to a gradual decline in Denisovan numbers, ultimately resulting in their extinction.

The extinction of the Denisovans, therefore, is not a simple tale of disappearance but a gradual process of integration and adaptation. Their genetic legacy, found in the DNA of millions of people today, is a testament to their enduring impact on the human story. Denisovans did not simply vanish; they became part of us, their genes living on and influencing traits in contemporary human populations. Their ability to adapt and their contributions to our genetic makeup highlight the interconnectedness of human evolution. The story of Denisovan extinction is one of transformation rather than eradication, reflecting the complex dynamics of human evolution where extinction often means assimilation and continuity in new forms. This process of integration has left a lasting imprint on the genetic diversity of modern humans, demonstrating the profound ways in which Denisovans continue to shape our biological heritage.

Estimating the exact time of Denisovan extinction remains challenging, with various pieces of evidence suggesting different timelines. It is commonly believed that Denisovans became extinct around 40,000 years ago, with other estimates placing their extinction closer to 30,000 years ago. Some recent studies even suggest that Denisovans might have survived until as recently as 15,000 years ago. The lack of clarity in their extinction date highlights the ongoing nature of paleoanthropological research and the need for further discoveries. What is likely, however, is that Denisovans were the last members of the Homo genus to coexist with Homo sapiens, making their survival story a significant chapter in the history of human evolution.

As we learn more about Denisovans through ongoing research and discoveries, we gain a deeper understanding of their role in our shared history. The study of their remains, tools, and genetic material continues to reveal the complexity of their existence and their interactions with other human species. This knowledge enriches our understanding of human evolution, illustrating the intricate web of connections that define our past. Each new discovery adds a layer of depth to our comprehension of Denisovan life, shedding light on their sophisticated culture, survival strategies, and their ultimate fate. The continuous exploration of Denisovan sites and the analysis of genetic data help to paint a fuller picture of their contributions to human history, emphasizing their significance in the broader context of our evolutionary journey.

The story of the Denisovans is a profound reminder of the resilience and adaptability of human beings. Though they disappeared as a distinct group, their legacy lives on in us. Through their contributions to our genetic heritage and their role in the broader narrative of human evolution, Denisovans continue to shape our understanding of what it means to be human. They are a testament to the interconnectedness of all human species, and their story is a crucial part of our own. The

Denisovans live through us, their genes a lasting legacy of their presence and impact on our evolutionary journey. Their story is not one of extinction but of transformation and continuity, reflecting the enduring impact of their existence on the genetic and cultural fabric of modern human populations. The legacy of the Denisovans, preserved in the DNA of millions, continues to influence our biology, culture, and understanding of human evolution, ensuring that their presence is felt long after their physical disappearance. As we delve deeper into the history of human evolution, the Denisovans stand as a powerful symbol of our shared heritage and the intricate web of connections that bind all human species.

Conclusion

The Denisovans, our second closest cousins, have left an indelible mark on the narrative of human evolution. Throughout this book, we have delved into their sophisticated technological innovations, remarkable geographic dispersal, unique biological adaptations, and complex social structures. These aspects of Denisovan life have highlighted their significance in our shared evolutionary journey. The Denisovans' ability to adapt to diverse environments and develop advanced cognitive and cultural practices underscores their vital role in the broader tapestry of human history. Their interbreeding with other hominins, including modern humans, has left a lasting genetic legacy that continues to shape modern human populations, particularly in Asia and Oceania. This genetic contribution enriches our understanding of the interconnectedness and complexity of human evolution.

The extinction of the Denisovans, likely occurring around 40,000 years ago, reflects a gradual process of integration and adaptation rather than complete disappearance. The combined effects of climate change and competition with Homo sapiens likely played significant roles in their decline. As the climate warmed and habitats transformed, Denisovans faced increasing pressure to adapt to new conditions while competing for resources with other human species. Despite these challenges, the Denisovans' genetic legacy lives on, highlighting their enduring impact on our species. Their story is not one of simple extinction but of transformation, where their genetic traits have been absorbed and continue to influence contemporary human populations. This process of genetic blending underscores the fluid boundaries between different human species and the profound ways in which Denisovans continue to shape our biological heritage.

As research on Denisovans progresses, our understanding of their role in human evolution continues to grow. The study of their remains, tools, and genetic material reveals the complexity of their existence and their interactions with other human species. This ongoing exploration enriches our knowledge of their sophisticated culture, survival strategies, and ultimate fate. The Denisovans exemplify the resilience and adaptability that characterize the human spirit. Despite the competition they faced, we likely shared food, tools, homes, and even love with them, highlighting the shared experiences that define our evolutionary journey. The study of Denisovans only began in earnest in 2010, and as we continue to uncover more about them, we can expect our appreciation for their contributions to human evolution to grow. The Denisovans live through us, their genes a lasting legacy of their presence and impact on our evolutionary journey. As we delve deeper into the history of human evolution, the Denisovans stand as a powerful symbol of our shared heritage and the intricate web of connections that bind all human species. Their story enriches our understanding of what it means to be human and underscores the profound interconnectedness of our shared past.

The Next Book

"Neanderthals: Our Closest Relatives"

Our journey into the past does not end here. This book is the fourth in a six-part series that delves into the fascinating journey of our ancient ancestors. Each book will uncover the mysteries and marvels of different hominin species, building a comprehensive picture of human evolution.

In the next book, we will turn our focus to one of the most well-known yet still enigmatic species: the Neanderthals. The upcoming book, "Neanderthals: Our Closest Relatives," will explore their advanced tools, social structure, art, religion, and more. We will address the most common questions about our relationship with Neanderthals, including theories about whether they enslaved early modern humans and if Homo sapiens were the primary cause of their extinction.

In this next book, we will discuss all these remarkable aspects and more, delving into the mysteries and marvels of the Neanderthals and their place in our shared human history.
Continue your exploration with "Neanderthals: Our Closest Relatives" and discover the next chapter in the incredible saga of human evolution.

Glossary of Terms

Archaic Humans:
- Early forms of human species that are anatomically distinct from modern humans but closely related, such as Neanderthals and Denisovans.

Cranial Capacity:
- The volume of the interior of the skull, which houses the brain; often used as an indicator of brain size and cognitive abilities.

DNA Sequencing:
- The process of determining the precise order of nucleotides within a DNA molecule, used to study genetic relationships and evolutionary history.

Fossil Record:
- The total number of fossils that have been discovered, as well as the information derived from them, providing evidence of past life forms and their evolution.

Genetic Legacy:
- The genetic information passed down from one generation to the next, which can provide insights into ancestral relationships and evolutionary history.

Interbreeding:
- The breeding between different species or populations, which can result in the exchange of genetic material and traits.

Neanderthals:
- An extinct species of archaic humans who lived in Europe and western Asia, closely related to modern humans, with whom they interbred.

Paleoanthropology:
- The scientific study of human evolution through the analysis of fossils and other remains.

Robust Build:
- Refers to a strong, sturdy physical structure, often associated with high levels of physical strength and durability.

Symbolic Behavior:
- Actions or creations that convey specific meanings within a culture, such as art, language, and rituals.

Evolutionary Pressure:
- Factors in the environment that influence reproductive success in individuals, leading to evolutionary change in populations.

Genetic Analysis:
- The study of DNA to understand genetic relationships, evolutionary history, and hereditary traits.

Skeletal Structure:
- The framework of bones and cartilage that supports and protects the body of an organism, providing insight into its physical capabilities and lifestyle.

References

Books:

"Masters of the Planet: The Search for Our Human Origins" by Ian Tattersall (St. Martin's Press)

"The Complete World of Human Evolution" by Chris Stringer and Peter Andrews (Thames & Hudson)

YouTube Channels: "North 02" & "PBS Eons"

Articles and Journals:

"Denisovan Ancestry and Population History" by David Reich et al. (Nature)

"Mum's a Neanderthal, Dad's a Denisovan: First Discovery of an Ancient-Human Hybrid" by Slon et al. (Nature)

"Denisovans, Neanderthals, and Early Modern Humans: A Review of the Pleistocene Hominin Fossils from the Altai Mountains" by Kuhlwilm et al. (Journal of Archaeological Research)